THE
BAR CART
BIBLE

EVERYTHING YOU NEED TO STOCK YOUR HOME BAR
and Make Delicious Classic Cocktails

Adams Media

NEW YORK   LONDON   TORONTO   SYDNEY   NEW DELHI

Adams Media
An Imprint of Simon & Schuster, Inc.
100 Technology Center Drive
Stoughton, MA 02072

For information about special discounts for bulk purchases, please contact Simon & Schuster Special Sales at 1-866-506-1949 or business@simonandschuster.com.

The Simon & Schuster Speakers Bureau can bring authors to your live event. For more information or to book an event contact the Simon & Schuster Speakers Bureau at 1-866-248-3049 or visit our website at www.simonspeakers.com.

Interior design by Colleen Cunningham. Interior images © annatigra/123RF. Insert images © jonathansloane, donfiore/Getty Images

Manufactured in the United States of America

10 2023

Library of Congress Cataloging-in-Publication Data
Adams Media (Firm), author.
The bar cart bible / Adams Media.
Avon, Massachusetts: Adams Media, 2017.
Includes bibliographical references and index.
LCCN 2016036834 | ISBN 9781507201169 (pob) | ISBN 1507201168 (pob) | ISBN 9781507201176 (ebook) | ISBN 1507201176 (ebook)
LCSH: Cocktails. | BISAC: COOKING / Beverages / Bartending. | COOKING / Beverages / Wine & Spirits.
LCC TX951 .B233 2017 | DDC 641.87/4--dc23
LC record available at https://lccn.loc.gov/2016036834

ISBN 978-1-5072-0116-9
ISBN 978-1-5072-0117-6 (ebook)

Contains material adapted from Bartender's Guide by John K. Waters, copyright © 2006 by Simon & Schuster, Inc., ISBN: 978-1-59869-764-3, and The Everything® Bartender's Book, 4th Edition, by Cheryl Charming, copyright © 2015 by Simon & Schuster, Inc., ISBN: 978-1-4405-8633-0.

These recipes were created for adults aged twenty-one and older, and are not intended to promote the excessive consumption of alcohol. Alcohol, when consumed to excess, can directly or indirectly result in permanent injury or death. The author, Adams Media, and Simon & Schuster, Inc. do not accept liability for any injury, loss, legal consequence, or incidental or consequential damage incurred by reliance on the information provided in this book.

Many of the designations used by manufacturers and sellers to distinguish their products are claimed as trademarks. Where those designations appear in this book and Simon & Schuster, Inc., was aware of a trademark claim, the designations have been printed with initial capital letters.

Contents

Introduction

*D*o you hate looking through cabinets for your bar equipment when all you want is a cocktail in-hand? Do you mean to impress your friends with a perfectly blended drink? Are you ready to be a fully equipped home bartender? If so, you need a bar cart to keep you organized and ready to mix up that cocktail whenever you like. The bar cart is a vintage staple with contemporary appeal: a lovely household focal point that is also just big enough to hold what you need to make yourself that perfect drink. Whether you use a rolling cart that can be wheeled from one room to another or a cabinet that remains stationary in the same corner for years, a bar cart is a perfect tool for keeping your drink-making supplies neatly corralled and easy to use.

A carefully curated and stocked bar cart allows you to be a relaxed host. And your guests will be able to serve themselves without fumbling through your kitchen cupboards and asking where you keep the limes. Imagine having everything you need to keep the party going right at your fingertips! Whether you're mixing for one, two, or a crowd, the information in this book is what you need to set up the perfect bar cart.

You'll find out exactly what tools, equipment, and ingredients you'll need to set up your cart. And you'll find more than 350 different drink recipes sure to please your guests (and yourself), and all can be directly served from your bar cart. The recipes range from the classics and historic cocktails to modern and contemporary cocktails found in craft bars of today.

As the bartender and host of a home party, it's your job to keep the good times rollin'—and with this book you'll be prepared. The book begins with a quick look at the history of the cocktail, then goes on to give you all the basics for concocting them. You'll find that there's no great mystery to making a cocktail. You only need to grasp the differences between drink families and the basics of shaking, blending, and mixing drinks. With the help of this book, you'll learn how to focus on the essentials—picking and choosing the right ingredients to keep your bar cart properly stocked. Plus you get an in-depth look at everything from glassware to garnishes.

For the sake of understanding—and sampling—the basic contents of drinks, a chapter is devoted to each spirit that makes cocktails possible: vodka, gin, rum, tequila, and whiskey. Some of the greatest drinks ever invented are made with one liquor and one mixer, and you'll find them in their respective chapters.

To get the most out of your bar cart, you have to be hip to what's current and wise enough to know what's classic. And this book gives you the best of what's timeless—the Whiskey Sour, Tom Collins, Old-Fashioned, and other favorites, complete with their variations and mutations.

Other chapters include shots and shooters, specialty and multi-spirit drinks, beer and wine cocktails, holiday drinks and punches, and mocktail (nonalcoholic) drinks.

This book will help you decide exactly what you need to host the memorable gatherings that friends will talk about for years to come—all kept within the space of your bar cart!

Part One.

Putting Together Your Bar Cart

01. Cocktails 101

*A*lcohol consumption dates almost back to the dawn of human civilization. Through it all, someone was always on hand to host and serve the alcohol. The duty of tending bar truly reaches back to ancient times. Understanding the role of the bartender as well as how drinks fall into various categories will help you devise the best approach for setting up a bar cart that's perfect for you.

MODERN BEGINNINGS

The popular alcohol brands we know today began to appear on the scene in the eighteenth century. In 1759, Arthur Guinness signed a 9,000-year lease for a brewery in Dublin. Richard Hennessy founded the Hennessy cognac distillery in 1765. Across the Atlantic, some historians claim that the Reverend Elijah Craig created a new whiskey formula of corn, rye, and barley malt, and established the Jim Beam distillery in 1789.

The origin of the word *cocktail* will probably never be known because there are many stories of where it came from. These origination accounts include

> **Definition of a Bartender**
>
> Bartender (*bär´ ten dur*) n. One who mixes and serves alcoholic drinks at a bar, lounge, or tavern. Also called barkeeper, barkeep, barmaid, barman, tavern keeper, whiskey slinger, mixologist, and tapster. Bartending basics start with the lingo.

those of a woman named Betsy Flanagan who put a rooster tail in drinks (cock-tail); an American tavern keeper who poured alcohol into a ceramic rooster, then guests would tap the tail when they wanted a drink; and a possible derivation from the French word *coquetel*. The very first known mention of the word cocktail was found in an early American newspaper, the *Farmer's Cabinet*, on April 28, 1803. It read, "Drank a glass of cocktail— excellent for the head. . . . Call'd at the Doct's. found Burnham—he looked very wise—drank another glass of cocktail."

Modern Cocktails

In the 1990s the production of high-end beer, wine, and spirits raised the cocktail bar, so to speak. Bartenders began making higher-quality cocktails that were superior to those created by bar chefs and mixologists at the turn of the century. Today you'll find bartenders who specialize in blowing fire, flipping bottles, dancing half-naked on a bar top, and using only fresh ingredients. However, all of this innovation did not necessarily affect the reliable average Joe barkeep down the street at your local watering hole. Just know that the majority of bartenders are the latter.

THE HOME-PARTY BARTENDER

The bartender can literally make or break a party. By keeping your bar cart well stocked and well organized, once everything is in place you can relax and just be the life of the party. You will not have to hassle with hunting down glasses, finding a place to stash bottles, and figuring out where to keep the garnishes. The home-party bartender's main job is to smile, be happy, and set the tone for the party. The bar cart can help make this a reality.

Keeping It Clean

Always think of sanitation. Don't let fingers touch drinking surfaces—the top of the straw, the rim of a glass, the ice, and the tops of bottles.

THE FIVE DRINK FAMILIES

It can be mind-boggling for the bartending novice to glance through cocktail recipes. But here is an insider tip: they really only break down into five categories—juicy, creamy, sour, hot, and carbonated. There are a few extensions of these categories, notably the tropical, highball, stick, and classic variations.

JUICY: Juicy drinks are made with any type of cold juice. Popular examples are Screwdriver, Cape Codder, and Bloody Mary.

CREAMY: Creamy drinks use cream, half-and-half, Irish cream, and similar liquids to give them a heavier texture. Popular examples are White Russian, Mudslide, Creamsicle, Grasshopper, and Bushwhacker.

SOUR: Sour drinks are made with the tang of citrus juice. Popular examples are Whiskey Sour, Amaretto Sour, Tom Collins, Margarita, Sour Appletini, and Long Island Iced Tea.

HOT: These are made with coffee, hot apple cider, tea, hot chocolate, and other similar hot beverages. Popular examples are Irish Coffee, Hot Toddy, Keoke Coffee, and Coffee Liqueur and Coffee.

CARBONATED: Carbonated drinks take advantage of soda's fizzy bubbles. These are basic highballs like Vodka and Soda, Vodka and Tonic, Gin and Tonic, Rum and Coke, Bourbon and Coke, and Seven and Seven.

If you know which of these five types of drinks you and your friends are most likely to enjoy, then you can stock your bar cart appropriately. Also, think seasonally. For example, in the winter, when hot drinks are appreciated, you may want to keep a coffeemaker nearby or add an insulated container for hot cocoa to the cart.

BARTENDING TERMS

If you grasp these following techniques, you'll be able to stand proud behind the bar with confidence.

BLENDED COCKTAIL: This is the type that you mix in a blender. Some people call it a frozen drink. The trick is to not put too much ice into the blender in the beginning; you can always add more to reach the desired consistency.

BUILT COCKTAIL: This one is the easiest to make. Start with a glass of ice. Pour in your spirits and follow with the mixer. You're done. You've made a drink "on the rocks."

CHILLED COCKTAIL: To chill cocktail glasses you can either squeeze them into the refrigerator next to the eggs or place them in the freezer next to the ice cream. But if you're serving directly from a bar cart, fill a glass with ice and water to chill it before you mix the drink. Beer should be served chilled, as should white wine: You can serve these from your refrigerator, or from an ice bucket or cooler.

FLAMED COCKTAIL: The most popular flamed drinks are topped with 151 proof rum, taking advantage of its flammability. Always use extreme caution when handling fire, and make sure the flame is blown out before consuming the drink.

FLOAT: To float means to pour some alcohol on top of a drink. The float adds flavor and character to a drink. Don't confuse it with the layered drink. The quantity of alcohol

> **Highballs**
>
> Originally, when a guest walked up to the bar and asked for a highball, the bartender grabbed a bottle of rye whiskey and mixed it with ginger ale. Today a highball just means a drink containing a spirit mixed with a carbonated mixer.

used in a float is less than that required for a layered drink. About half an ounce will suffice.

LAYERED DRINK: Different types of alcohol have different weights (densities). This allows them to be layered on top of one another. Pour the spirit onto something like a bar spoon to break its fall so that it goes into the glass slowly. This way it layers on top of the spirit layer below.

MUDDLED COCKTAIL: To muddle is to crush ingredients to release their flavors.

NEAT DRINK: Neat is to pour straight from the bottle into a glass. Ice or mixers are not added.

ROLLED COCKTAIL: Build a drink then pour the contents into another glass or shaker tin, and then return it to the original glass.

SHAKEN COCKTAIL: Put ice and drink ingredients in a shaker tin and shake the drink to make it cold.

STRAINED COCKTAIL: Chill the drink and then strain it over ice or straight up. The most popular use of this method is with straight-up shots and shooters. The term straight up refers to something that is chilled and served without ice.

STIRRED COCKTAIL: One stirring technique is to build a cocktail and then stir it with a straw. The other way is used when you're making, for example, a classic Manhattan or Martini: You fill a bar glass (pint glass) with ice, pour in your ingredients, stir with a bar spoon, and strain.

The recipes in this book tell you if the drink should be shaken, stirred, layered, and so forth. These terms will also be helpful to know when a guest has a special order—or if you just want to show off your bartending knowledge!

02. Bar Cart Equipment

*T*hough a bar cart can be a simple, low-key way to corral a few bottles of spirits, a carefully stocked cart—one with the right tools and equipment—can make mixing drinks a pleasure instead of a necessary chore. Think of your bar cart as the toolbox of the bartending trade. What goes in it should be thought out ahead of time. Your personal preferences (and those of your friends) are more important than what any cocktail guide tells you. If you like drinking your highballs out of martini glasses, then who are we to stop you? Even so, you should devote some time to planning and acquiring the right equipment for your cart.

GLASSWARE

Almost as important as what is in the drink is what the drink is in. And this isn't just about aesthetics. Glassware has a big influence on how the drink works—whether its flavor is enhanced or harmed.

The glassware you choose for your bar cart depends on your personal drink preferences. In general, the most popular glasses to keep on hand are

Stemless versus Stemmed

In some cases there are essential reasons for the choice of glass. A cocktail glass is held by its stem so that the hand does not warm the drink. A brandy snifter is rested in the palm, so the hand warms the liquid and releases its aroma.

the cocktail glass, the highball glass, and the shot glass. If you have a lot of wine drinkers in the crowd, you'll want to keep a few wine glasses on hand. Unless you are very picky about your wine, you don't need to keep separate glasses for red and white wines.

The **PINT GLASS** can also be used as a mixing glass or all-purpose glass. Beer, specialty drinks, or tropical drinks may all be served in a pint glass.

BRANDY SNIFTERS range considerably in size, from 5 to 25 ounces, so use your personal preference as a guide. The brief stem allows your hand to warm the brandy. The mouth of the snifter, narrower than the base, holds the aroma. Cordials and liqueurs can be served in them, as well as high-end single malt Scotch, whiskey, rum, and tequila.

CHAMPAGNE GLASSES come in different styles, a 4- to 6-ounce stemmed, wide-mouthed glass (coupe), or a 7- to 8-ounce flute. The style does make a difference. The open surface of the wide-mouthed glass allows the carbonation to escape, while the narrow flute preserves the bubbles. There are also two styles of flutes, called tulip and trumpet (named for their shape).

The Stemmed Boob?

It's an urban legend that the coupe-style champagne glass was modeled after Marie Antoinette's breasts so that everyone could drink from them. However, this cannot be true because this style glass was invented in the 1600s and Marie wasn't born until the 1700s.

The **COCKTAIL GLASS** is the symbol of drinking establishments throughout the world. Its size ranges between 4 to 12 ounces and comes in many vintage and modern shapes. The larger-sized glasses are meant for cocktails made with added mixers like an Apple Ginger Gin. Smaller cocktail glasses are meant for spirit-only cocktails like a Classic Martini.

A **HIGHBALL GLASS**, the most universally used glass, holds 8 to 12 ounces. It is used for on-the-rocks drinks (highballs) like Scotch and Soda, or Gin and Tonic. It is also used for other two-ingredient, on-the-rocks drinks like a Fuzzy Navel or Moscow Mule.

The **IRISH COFFEE MUG** is a soul-warming glass container for all hot drinks. At 6 to 8 ounces, it offers enough volume for the right proportions of spirits and nonalcoholic ingredients, and its handle allows you to hold the glass while the drink is still properly hot.

A **LIQUEUR GLASS** is also known as a cordial glass or a pony. You'll find them in different shapes, but they all hold 1 ounce of liquid.

Irish Coffee History

Joe Sheridan, an Irish airport bartender, invented the Irish Coffee at what is now Shannon Airport in Ireland. In 1952, a San Francisco reporter named Stanton Delaplane took the recipe back to Jack Koeppler, who owned the Buena Vista Cafe. Today, the bar claims to serve 2,000 Irish Coffees a day.

The **OLD-FASHIONED GLASS** is for the venerable Old-Fashioned, but it's also used for most cocktails on the rocks (hence its alias, the rocks glass). Ranging from 4 to 8 ounces, the old-fashioned is the short, squat member of the glass team.

A 3- to 4-ounce **SHERRY GLASS** holds many of the before- and after-dinner drinks, such as sherry, port, and various aperitifs. These are, by definition, small drinks, so the smaller size of the glass suits them.

The 1- or 2-ounce **SHOT GLASS** does double duty as a measurer and a serving glass.

 The 8- to 20-ounce **RED WINE GLASS** is balloon-shaped (left); the 8- to 20-ounce **WHITE WINE GLASS** is quite a bit slimmer (right).

TOOLS OF THE TRADE

Chances are you already have a number of the basic bar cart tools: a paring knife and cutting board, a corkscrew and a strainer. But no well-equipped bar would be without a few essential specialty utensils. As you equip your bar cart, think about the drinks you and your guests like the most. This will help you prioritize which tools to purchase. For example, if you don't often use juice as a mixer, there's no need to keep a juice extractor on hand.

BAR SPOON. A bar spoon is used to stir classic Manhattans and Martinis and other cocktails in a mixing glass. It is also used to layer drinks.

 BLENDER. If frozen Daiquiris are your drink, you'll need to keep a blender on your bar cart. But unless you serve a lot of frozen drinks, the real estate is better reserved for other tools.

CORKSCREW. The professional corkscrew (wine tool, pictured) is the "waiter's" version, a two-in-one gadget that opens wine and beer bottles. If your corkscrew does not also include a bottle opener, keep one on your bar cart, too.

ICE SCOOP. An ice scoop keeps bacteria-infested hands out of the ice. The 24-ounce size is good but you can get away with something smaller if your ice bucket is scaled down to fit on your bar cart.

 **JIGGER.** This measuring device is double-sided with different measures on each end. The most popular has 1½ ounces on one side and ½ ounce on the other, but you can buy many other sizes to meet your needs.

JUICE EXTRACTOR AND CITRUS REAMER. Using an extractor or a reamer is the most common way to get fresh juice when making a cocktail.

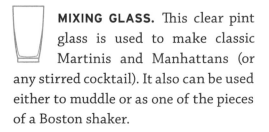 **MIXING GLASS.** This clear pint glass is used to make classic Martinis and Manhattans (or any stirred cocktail). It also can be used either to muddle or as one of the pieces of a Boston shaker.

> **Using the Waiter's Version Corkscrew**
>
> This is the only corkscrew a real bartender uses. Here's how to use it to open a wine bottle. With the knife of the corkscrew, remove the foil around the top of the cork. Insert the screw (worm) into the center of the cork and twist until it's nearly all the way into the cork. Set the pry bar on the lip of the bottle and pull the cork straight up. The knife will also come in handy for many things when working as a bartender.

MUDDLER. This stick can be made of wood, plastic, or a combination of materials. It's used to crush mint, sugar, fruit, and herbs.

POUR SPOUTS. Pour spouts are pushed into bottle openings, allowing the speed-pouring of liquor and liqueurs. After a party, simply take them out and put the caps back on the bottles.

SHAKER TINS. There are two types of shaker tins: cobbler and Boston. The cobbler shakers consist of three pieces—a tumbler, a lid with a built-in strainer, and a cap to cover the strainer. These are popular among home bartenders because they are easy to use. The Boston shaker consists of two pieces that fit inside each other. One piece is stainless steel, and the other piece is either a smaller stainless steel tin or a mixing glass. You shake your drink, then tap where they meet to break the seal and pour the drink. The two-part design allows for quicker pouring.

STRAINER. There are three types of strainers: the Hawthorne (pictured), the julep, and a conical mesh strainer. The handheld conical mesh strainer is used in conjunction with the Hawthorne strainer as a double strainer (strain with the Hawthorne strainer into the mesh strainer). The Hawthorne has a coil around it and is used with a shaker tin. The julep strainer is placed in a convex position inside a mixing glass.

ZESTER. A zester (also called a channel knife) makes long curly twists out of citrus fruit peel. Simply set the zester on the fruit, apply pressure, and slice off a long piece.

03. Bar Cart Ingredients

*M*arines, Boy Scouts, and bartenders should always be prepared. Stocking a bar cart should be a matter of personal taste, lifestyle, and finances. But unless having a drink is always going to be a solitary pleasure, you should be prepared for guests. That means keeping them in mind as you stock the ingredients for your party.

For many, planning a cocktail party can be downright nerve-racking. But if you've stocked your bar cart with the basics, and you have the right tools, glasses, and mixers, the refreshments, at least, should be a breeze.

You can never fully anticipate what your guests will want to drink, but they will tend to be satisfied with a basic variety—after all, this is your home, not a bar. That said, a thoughtfully curated bar cart can handle a cocktail party of most any size.

THE BAR CART BASICS

A basic bar for a bar cart includes:

- Bourbon
- Brandy
- Gin
- Rum
- Scotch
- Tequila
- Vodka
- Whiskey (Irish)
- Blended Whiskey or Rye

If you have beer drinkers and/or wine drinkers in your crowd, you may want to delete some of the spirits (such as brandy) and refine the similar spirits (bourbon, scotch, whiskey, blended whiskey) into just one or two choices in total.

MIXERS

Mixers provide the flavor and balance that combine with liquor to give a drink its distinctive taste. Mixers range from plain water to club soda, and from flavored sodas to fruit juices.

Popular mixers include orange juice, cranberry juice, pineapple juice, grapefruit juice, lemon and lime juices, olive juice, V8 vegetable juice, tomato juice, simple syrup, grenadine, coconut cream, honey, gomme, orgeat, lime juice cordial, hot sauce, Worcestershire, beef bouillon, Clamato juice, clam juice, milk, cream, half-and-half, ice cream, hot chocolate, unsalted butter, eggnog, egg white, all sodas, coffee, espresso, tea, and hot water.

You can buy prepared mixes for Daiquiris, Margaritas, and Bloody Marys, among others. They come in bottled and powdered form. Some are excellent and some are not. Try a few out and select your favorites.

Your curated bar cart could include a few select sodas, one or two fruit juices, and a cocktail mix or two.

CONDIMENTS: THE LITTLE THINGS IN LIFE

Condiments make all the difference. Stocking the bar cart with them should be as basic as buying the liquor, and most of them won't take up much room on your cart. A collection of condiments is dependent on personal needs, but here are some condiments you can try:

- ◯ Cocoa powder
- ◯ Cinnamon
- ◯ Cayenne or chili pepper
- ◯ Coconut flakes
- ◯ Sugar—brown, raw, or cubes
- ◯ Salt—kosher or celery
- ◯ Pepper—black or white pepper

Sugar

Sugar is a powerful partner in many drinks, but its presence should be behind the scenes, never tasted distinctly, and never felt as granules. Unless granulated sugar is specified, confectioners' sugar, referred to in this book as fine sugar, should be used.

GARNISHES

A Gibson is not a Gibson without its pearl onion garnish, and a Martini is just not the same without the olive. The most popular garnishes are the lime, lemon, cherry, and olive. Keeping these available at your bar cart will satisfy most drinkers.

Cutting Garnishes

Cutting garnishes can be intimidating for some people, but it's really easy. Just make sure you always wash your hands well first or wear rubber gloves when handling garnishes. After making a cut, always lay the flat side of the fruit down to create a stable base for cutting.

THE WEDGE: To cut the essential wedge, slice a lime (or lemon) in half lengthwise and cut each half into four wedges. When serving, squeeze the juice into the drink, rub the fruit side around the rim of the glass, and drop the slice in.

THE SLICE: If you prefer to set the fruit on the edge of the glass, cut it into eighths and make a slit in the meat of each slice.

THE QUARTER: Quarter cuts work best when muddling. Cut the fruit in half through the middle. Lay both pieces flat and then cut twice, making a cross. This will yield four quarters per piece.

THE WHEEL: Cut off the ends of the fruit, then cut a ¼"-deep slit lengthwise (this slit makes it easy for you to set it on the rim of the glass). Hold the fruit firmly and cut 4 or 5 wheels.

THE ZEST: The zest is the cut that really helps you show off. It's an oval-shaped rind slice from a piece of citrus. The zest can be squeezed over a drink, or it can be combined with a flame to make an attention-getting burst. This burst happens because the oil of the rind meets the flame. Most often the zest is made from an orange. Don't confuse this with the kind of zesting done to citrus fruits in cooking and baking. That type of zesting results in bitty shreds of peel

Be Bitter!

While the sound of bitters is not appealing, the little bottles contain a wonderful witch's brew of roots and barks, berries, and herbs. Bitters add a kick of flavor to the mixed drinks they accompany, always in small amounts—dashes, to be approximately exact. The most common type of bitters is Angostura, made in Trinidad. Two that are sometimes used are Peychaud's, from New Orleans, and Regans' orange bitters. Bitters do have an alcohol content and should not be served to anyone who abstains totally. Tasting them plain is not recommended, either.

that nobody would want floating in a drink.

THE TWIST: There are a few ways to make twists (usually lemon). One is to cut off both ends of the fruit so the inside meat shows. Make a slit in the fruit from end to end. Squeeze a bar spoon beneath the skin and scoop out the fruit. Cut the peel widthwise into ¼" strips. Another technique is to cut slits all around a whole citrus fruit and cut off one end. You can then peel off a twist to order. The proper way to garnish with a twist is to twist the peel, colored side down, over the drink, so the oils will release. Then, rub the colored side around the rim and drop the twist into the drink. You can use a zester to make a long curly twist. Simply set the zester on the fruit's peel, apply pressure, and slice off a long piece.

> **Rimming**
>
> Glass rims can be dipped in something wet or sticky and then dipped into something edible. Rimming always makes a great presentation. Margaritas look better with kosher salt around their rims, and Chocolate Martinis are more appetizing in chocolate-rimmed glasses.

Test out these variations so you're ready to show your skill and add a bit of style to your cocktails, no matter what's on order!

MEASUREMENTS MATTER

Since the metric system measures the world, except in the United States, here are some equivalents and charts to help you avoid confusion. When measuring ingredients for a drink, remember that the balance is important. To make weaker or stronger drinks, adjust all of the components accordingly.

BARTENDER MEASURES

Bar Measurements	Standard	Metric
1 dash	0.03 ounce	0.9 milliliter
1 splash	0.25 ounce	7.5 milliliters
1 teaspoon	0.125 ounce	3.7 milliliters
1 tablespoon	0.375 ounce	11.1 milliliters
1 float	0.5 ounce	14.8 milliliters
1 pony	1 ounce	29.5 milliliters
1 jigger	1.5 ounces	44.5 milliliters
1 cup	8 ounces	237 milliliters
1 pint	16 ounces	472 milliliters
1 quart	32 ounces	946 milliliters
1 gallon	128 ounces	3.78 liters

METRIC SIZES FOR SPIRITS, BEER, AND WINES

Name of Container	Standard	Metric
split	6.3 ounces	187 milliliters
half	12.6 ounces	375 milliliters
fifth	25.3 ounces	750 milliliters
quart	33.8 ounces	1 liter
magnum	50.7 ounces	1.5 liters
jeroboam	101.4 ounces	3 liters
nebuchadnezzar	3.96 gallons	15 liters
keg	7.75 gallons	29.3 liters

These measures are great to look up when having a cocktail party. The main things to keep in mind are that you can get three or four servings from a bottle of wine, twenty to twenty-five shots of alcohol from a fifth (750 ml), and thirty to thirty-five shots of alcohol from a liter.

Part Two.

The Bar Cart Bible
Drink Recipes

04. Beer Cocktails

The Egyptians were the first to refine the texture and taste of beer. After that, the Greeks and Romans carried on the beer-making tradition when there weren't grapes to make wine. Ancient Germans (Teutons) took their beer very seriously, even using it as a sacrifice to their beer gods.

During medieval times, monastery monks focused intently on making the best beer possible. Hops were first used in the 1000s, and doing this must have improved the quality of beer tremendously because priests used it to baptized children. By the 1200s beer was classified as ale (top-fermenting) or lager (bottom-fermenting). Germany brewed cold-temperature lagers, storing them in caves, while England brewed room-temperature ales and stored them in cellars. In 1519, the Reinheitsgebot law was enacted in Bavaria, Germany, requiring that all beer be made only from barley, hops, and water. By the early 1600s a way to bottle beer with a cork was perfected, the most popular drinking song in England was "John Barleycorn," and there were more than 17,000 taverns in England alone.

In 1978, U.S. President Jimmy Carter signed a bill legalizing home brewing of beer for the first time since Prohibition. People began experimenting, making their own home brews. Handcrafted beer combined with a high-tech era, resulted in microbrews. Microbreweries sprouted up all over the country. Today, microbreweries producing craft beer are in every state.

Beer cocktails are libations that contain beer. Beer can be used as a base ingredient or as a substitution for a carbonated mixer. Using craft beers in cocktails enhances the flavor of a drink, and this allows people to get creative when combining flavors with other mixers and spirits.

Beer cocktails don't require a complicated set of instructions or much in the way of special techniques. The ingredients list for a beer cocktail is almost always quite small. And they're a good way to introduce your guests to the wonders of beverages beyond beer.

Baltimore Zoo

½ ounce vodka

½ ounce rum

½ ounce grenadine

Stout to fill glass

Pour the ingredients into a pint glass.

Beer Buster

2 ounces vodka

14 ounces light beer

Pour the vodka into a chilled glass and add the beer.

> **Two Types of Beer**
>
> Beer is classified as ale or lager. Ale is made by adding yeast on top of the brewing mixture. Types of ales include stout, porter, bitter, wheat, lambic, brown, pale, Belgian, barley wine, amber, and cream. Lager is made by adding yeast on the bottom of the brewing mixture. Types of lagers include bock, dry, light, ice, pilsner, and malt.

Beermato

2 ounces Clamato juice

½ ounce lemon juice

2 dashes Worcestershire sauce

12 ounces light beer

Pour the ingredients into a pint glass.

Bee Sting

12 ounces dark beer

3 ounces orange juice

Pour the beer into the glass then pour the orange juice into the beer. Stir gently to mix.

Bittersweet

1 ounce Campari

4 ounces orange soda

4 ounces light beer

Fill a highball glass with ice and add all the ingredients. Stir gently.

Black and Tan

8 ounces pale ale (such as Bass)

8 ounces stout (such as Guinness)

Pour the pale ale into the glass, then slowly pour the stout on top of the ale to create a layer. Use the back of a spoon to break the fall.

Black Shandy

8 ounces stout

8 ounces cola

Pour the ingredients into a pint glass. Make a Ginger Shandy by using equal parts ginger beer and light beer.

Black Velvet

6 ounces champagne or sparkling wine

6 ounces stout or dark porter

Float the stout on top of the champagne. Do not stir.

Popular Ales

The most popular ale brands are Bass, Red Hook, Guinness, Full Sail, Sierra Nevada, Pete's Wicked Ale, Pyramid Hefeweizen, Sam Adams Cream Stout, Sam Adams Cherry Wheat, and Sam Adams Boston Ale.

Bloody Beer

14 ounces lager

2 ounces Bloody Mary mix

Dash Tabasco (optional)

Dash Worcestershire (optional)

Pour the lager into the glass then pour the Bloody Mary mix into the beer. Embellish with a dash of Tabasco and a dash of Worcestershire if you like.

Blow My Skull Off

15 ounces stout

1 ounce rum

Dash cayenne pepper

1 lime slice

Pour the stout into the glass then pour the rum into the stout. Sprinkle the cayenne pepper in and mix gently. Squeeze the juice from the lime and drop it into the beer.

Boilermaker

15 ounces light beer

1 ounce whiskey

Combine the beer and whiskey in a pint glass using your preferred method (see sidebar).

Caribbean Night

15 ounces light beer

1 ounce coffee liqueur

Pour the beer into the glass then pour the coffee liqueur into the beer. Stir gently to mix thoroughly.

Dark Port

14 ounces stout

2 ounces port

Pour the ingredients into a pint glass.

Methods to Build a Boilermaker

The etiquettist Emily Post would sip this drink after pouring the shot into the beer (pinky finger raised). Other people might drop the shot, glass and all, into the filled beer mug and chug-a-lug before the foam hits the floor.

Depth Charge

2 ounces peppermint schnapps

14 ounces light beer

Pour the peppermint schnapps into a pint glass. Top off with beer.

Dr. Pepper

14 ounces light beer

1 ounce amaretto

½ ounce 151 rum

¼ ounce grenadine

Pour the beer into the glass then pour the amaretto, rum, and grenadine into the beer.

Jamaican Firefly

¾ ounce lime juice

1 ounce simple syrup

1½ ounces dark rum

2 ounces ginger beer

1 lime slice, for garnish (optional)

Combine the liquid ingredients in a shaker with ice. Shake well. Strain into a highball glass. Garnish with a lime slice.

Ale Characteristics

Stout: very dark (almost black) with a very full body. Brown ales: medium-bodied, buttery, and smooth. Porter: dark and hoppy. Wheat: light, creamy, and fruity. Pale ale: medium-bodied with a slight bitterness. Cream ale: light-bodied with a malty flavor. Amber: medium-bodied and hoppy.

Lagerita

1½ ounces tequila

1 ounce triple sec

1 ounce lime juice

Salt, for rim

16 ounces light Mexican beer

Combine the tequila, triple sec, and lime juice in a shaker with ice. Shake well. Strain into a tall, chilled, half-salted rimmed highball glass. Add the beer on top.

Light Lunch Box

11 ounces light beer

1 ounce amaretto

4 ounces orange juice

Pour the beer into the glass then add the amaretto and orange juice into the beer. Stir gently to mix.

Michelada

7 ounces light beer

1 ounce tequila

1 ounce lemon juice

Dash Tabasco

Dash Worcestershire

Pinch salt and pepper

Dash grenadine

Pour the beer into a pint glass of ice. Add the tequila, lemon juice, Tabasco, Worcestershire, and salt and pepper. Top with the grenadine.

Monaco

8 ounces lemon-lime soft drink (like 7Up)

8 ounces lager

Pour the ingredients into a pint glass in the order they're listed.

Orange-Spiked Lager

1 ounce triple sec liqueur

15 ounces light beer

Pour the orange liqueur into a glass. Fill with beer. To make the beer appear green, replace the orange liqueur with blue curaçao, which still has an orange flavor.

Peach-Spiked Brew

1 ounce peach schnapps

15 ounces light beer

Pour the peach schnapps into a glass. Fill with beer.

Raging Bull

12 ounces Mexican beer (like Corona or Pacifico)

3 ounces Red Bull

1 ounce tequila

Pour the ingredients into a pint glass.

The Five Steps in Making Beer

1. Harvest barley and soak it, allowing it to germinate to create malt.

2. Clean and grind malt, then optionally mix it with corn grits; cook to create wort.

3. Boil wort with the herb hops.

4. Cool wort and add either top- or bottom-fermenting yeast.

5. Add flavors, then filter and pasteurize. Store in cans, bottles, or kegs.

Red Eye

14 ounces lager

2 ounces tomato juice

1 lemon slice (optional)

Pour the beer into the glass then pour the tomato juice into the beer. You can embellish it with a lemon slice if you desire.

Red-Headed Stepchild

14 ounces light beer

1 ounce whiskey

½ ounce grenadine

Pour all ingredients into a glass. Gently mix.

Russian Ale

15 ounces stout

1 ounce vodka

Pour the ingredients into a pint glass.

Beer and Health Benefits

Many scientific studies on beer suggest it has health benefits. Beer makes bones stronger because of its high silicon levels. Beer prevents kidney stones in men. Moderate beer consumption lowers risk of heart disease, and those who do consume it moderately are less likely to develop high blood pressure.

Skip and Go Naked

½ ounce gin

½ ounce sweet-and-sour mix

Beer to fill

Shake the gin and sweet-and-sour mix with ice. Pour into a highball glass of ice. Fill with beer.

Skippy

2 ounces vodka

6 ounces lemonade

8 ounces lager

Pour the vodka and lemonade into a glass. Fill with the lager.

05. Wine Cocktails

*F*acing the forest of wine bottles at the liquor or grocery store can be daunting, but making sense of it is straightforward. The best way to learn about wine is to investigate and experiment yourself—in other words, pick a bottle that looks interesting and see what happens! Individual taste is the best standard for personal pleasure.

Here you will find recipes for cocktails made from still wines (the fermented reds and whites you normally think of as wine), sparkling wines (think champagne!), and distilled wines (such as brandy). Distilled wines are concentrated through the distillation process, giving them a higher alcohol content than fermented wines.

Curating your bar cart means keeping the number of bottles you have to juggle to a minimum. Don't feel you have to have bottles of reds, whites, sparkling, and distilled wines on hand. Select the ingredient that is most versatile for you (for some, that might be champagne; for others, it might be brandy) and keep that on your bar cart. Reducing clutter can also allow you to invest in better quality ingredients. Instead of buying several medium quality wines, buy one good quality wine.

Using wine in cocktails is a fun way to broaden your horizons and enjoy wine in a new way. And if that bottle you opened isn't quite your thing, you can always doctor it up with a few other ingredients from your bar cart.

Biblical Vineyards

The first written account of wine is in the Bible, which notes that Noah planted a vineyard and made wine. Before that, wine was probably discovered by accident due to grape spoilage. Researchers say that social wine drinking probably began around 6000 B.C.E. In some cultures, beer was for the villagers and workers and wine was reserved for royalty. The Romans are truly responsible for expanding the wine culture in the Old World, mainly due to the sheer size of the Roman Empire.

STILL WINES

White wines are served chilled and red wines are served at room temperature. Also, the name of a wine clues you in to the type of grapes used. For example, a Cabernet Sauvignon is made from Cabernet Sauvignon grapes.

Popular red wines include Cabernet Sauvignon (full-bodied and dark), Merlot (medium-bodied and lighter than Cabernet), Burgundy (heavy and dark), Beaujolais (light-bodied, with a better taste when chilled), Pinot Noir (light-bodied and mild), Zinfandel (medium-bodied and spicy), Petite Sirah (rich berry flavor), and Chianti (soft and smooth).

Popular white wines include Chardonnay (dry and crisp), Sauvignon Blanc (dry and citrusy), Chenin Blanc (fruity), Chablis (light and woody), Riesling (fruity and sweet), and Gewürztraminer (spicy sweet).

Aloha Bubbly

2 ounces pineapple juice

2 ounces club soda, more if needed

½ teaspoon sugar

2 ounces dry white wine

Add the first three ingredients to a highball glass. Add crushed ice and the white wine. Add additional club soda to fill and stir again.

Bishop

2 ounces orange juice

1 ounce lemon juice

1 teaspoon sugar

4 ounces red wine

Pour the juices and sugar into a mixing glass nearly filled with ice. Strain into a highball glass over ice. Fill with red wine.

Blue Sangria

4 ounces white wine

1 ounce blue curaçao

2 ounces white grape juice

2 ounces soda water

Fruit, for garnish

Fill a large white wine glass with ice and add the liquid ingredients. Garnish with fruit.

Wine Terms to Know

Aging = Effects of maturation

Alcoholic fermentation = The process by which yeast and sugar in grapes react to produce alcohol

AOC = Appellation d'origine contrôlée, the quality control designation on French wine

Claret = English term for red wine

Demi-Sec = Medium sweet

Doux = Sweet

Fortified wine = Wine with a high-strength spirit added

Cactus Berry

3 ounces merlot

1 ounce tequila

1 ounce Cointreau

1 ounce lime juice

1 lime wedge, for garnish

Combine the liquid ingredients in a shaker half filled with ice. Shake well. Strain into a cocktail glass. Garnish with lime wedge.

Rosy Navel

1 ounce peach schnapps

1 ounce orange juice

5 ounces rosé wine

2 ounces soda water

Fill a large white wine glass with ice and add all the ingredients. Stir.

No Rules for Sangria

There are no real rules for sangria except that it needs to have wine and fruit in it. You can easily add or substitute clear liquids such as white (clear) cranberry juice, white grape juice, champagne (for carbonation), and any seasonal fruits you desire. It's all up to you.

Valentine

4 ounces Beaujolais

2 ounces cranberry juice

Combine the ingredients in a shaker half filled with ice. Shake, then strain into a red wine glass.

Vino Crush

4 ounces white wine

1 ounce Grand Marnier

Orange soda to fill

Fill a highball glass with ice and pour in the wine and Grand Marnier. Fill with the orange soda.

White or Red Wine Cooler

5 ounces wine

Sprite or 7Up to fill

1 lemon or lime wedge, for garnish

Pour the wine and soda over ice into a large wine glass. Stir gently. Garnish with fruit wedge.

White or Red Wine Spritzer

5 ounces red or white wine

Club soda or sparkling water to fill

1 lemon or lime wedge, for garnish

Pour the wine and soda over ice into a large wine glass. Stir gently. Garnish with fruit wedge.

White Sangria

4 ounces white wine

1 ounce apple juice

¼ teaspoon ground cinnamon (optional)

Soda water or Perrier to fill

Sliced seasonal fruits, for garnish

Fill a large white wine glass with ice and add the liquid ingredients. Garnish with slices of seasonal fruits.

SPARKLING WINES

Champagne is sexy, no doubt about it. Its bubbles are flirtatious, and its fizz is a sparkling invitation to hold hands, sigh, and exchange glances.

The method for making champagne begins with a cuvée, a vineyard's blend of dry white wines. The blend is bottled with yeast and sugar for a second fermentation to create the bubbles. In the process a sediment is formed. Mon Dieu! No matter how fine the flavor, gunk in the bottle will not do. So the second step ingeniously collects the sediment. The bottles are tilted and turned so that the sediment clings to the cork. In the third step, the cork (along with the unsightly muck) is removed, a bit of sugar is added, and the bottle is recorked. The typical mushroom-shaped cork is a result of ramming two-thirds of a cork wider than the neck into the bottle. Under pressure, the cork forms a perfect seal. The wire on top is to prevent any over-exuberant bubbles from popping their cork.

> **Champagne versus Sparkling Wine**
>
> Champagne is a term often used to describe any sparkling wine, but that is technically incorrect. Genuine champagne is only produced in France, in the chalky hills and valleys near the Marne River that make up the Champagne region. But the champagne method (*méthode champenoise*) of fermenting wine in the bottle it is sold in can be used anywhere to make still wine sparkle.

Champagne offers choices and clear descriptions. Created in a range from dry to sweet, the contents of the bottles are conveniently labeled. Brut is very dry; extra dry or sec is not as dry; demi-sec is the half-and-half of champagne, slightly sweet and dry; and doux is the sweetest of all.

American Flyer

1½ ounces light rum

1 tablespoon lime juice

½ teaspoon simple syrup

Chilled champagne to fill

Combine the first three
ingredients in a shaker with ice.
Shake well. Strain into chilled
white wine glass. Fill with
champagne.

Champagne Antoine

1 ounce gin

1 ounce dry vermouth

⅛ ounce Pernod

Chilled dry champagne to fill

1 lemon twist

Shake the gin, vermouth, and
Pernod with ice. Strain into
a champagne flute. Fill with
champagne and add a lemon
twist.

Wine Words to Know

Jug wine = American term for
table wine

Sec = Dry

Tannin = Natural component
in skins, seeds, and stems
of grapes that creates a dry,
puckering sensation in the
mouth

Varietal = Grape variety;
wines made from a single
grape are varietals, and they
are labeled with the name of
that grape

Vintage = Defines the grape
harvest of a single year

Champagne Fizz

2 ounces gin

1 ounce lemon juice

1 teaspoon sugar

Chilled champagne to fill

Combine the gin, lemon juice,
and sugar in a shaker half filled
with ice. Shake well. Strain into
a highball glass over ice. Fill with
champagne.

Champagne Flamingo

¾ ounce vodka

¾ ounce Campari

Chilled champagne to fill

Zest of orange, for garnish

Shake vodka and Campari with ice and strain into a champagne flute. Fill with champagne. Garnish with zest of orange.

Bubbly Bath

Rumor has it that Marilyn Monroe once filled up her tub with 350 bottles of champagne and took a bath.

Flirtini

½ ounce vodka

1 ounce pineapple juice

Chilled champagne to fill

Shake the vodka and pineapple juice together. Strain into a champagne flute. Fill with champagne.

Origins of the French 75

The French 75 is believed to have been invented by legendary bartender Harry MacElhone in honor of the famous French 75 light field gun. The artillery piece was a major weapon in World War I, and the cocktail debuted in Paris after the Great War.

French 75

1 ounce gin

1 ounce lemon juice

½ ounce simple syrup

Chilled champagne to fill

1 lemon twist, for garnish

Build gin, lemon juice, and simple syrup into a champagne flute and top with chilled champagne. Garnish with lemon twist.

Mimosa

¼ of a champagne flute of freshly squeezed orange juice

Chilled champagne to fill

1 strawberry, for garnish (optional)

Fill a champagne flute a quarter of the way with orange juice. Fill with champagne and garnish the rim with a strawberry, if desired.

Poinsettia

½ ounce cranberry juice

¼ ounce triple sec

Chilled champagne to fill

1 lime twist, for garnish

Pour the juice and the triple sec in a champagne flute. Fill with chilled champagne and garnish with lime twist.

Serving Champagne

Keep the cork pointed away from anything it could hurt or break if it accidentally pops out (at 100 miles per hour!). Release the cork by gripping the cork tightly with one hand and twisting the bottom of the bottle with the other hand. You should hear a soft hiss and pop. To pour, hold the bottom of the bottle with your thumb into the punt (the dent in the bottom of the bottle) and your fingers spread underneath.

DISTILLED WINES

Cognac and brandy are distilled wines. All cognacs are brandy, but not all brandies are cognacs. Brandy can be made from any fruit (including grapes). Cognac must be made in the Cognac region of France from grapes grown in the same place. Cognacs are distilled twice and stored in oak casks made from the wood of the trees grown in the Cognac region. The length of the aging process varies and distillers offer a guide for the buyer.

Cognac Classifications

There are three general classifications to separate cognacs from each other—VS (very special, aged at least 2 years), VSOP (very special old pale or very superior old pale, aged at least 4 years), and XO (extra old, aged at least 6 years).

Aside from cognac, there are many types of brandies. The vintners of California distill brandies from their own grapes, which tend to be lighter and smoother. There is a dry Italian brandy called grappa; apple brandies such as calvados; kirschwasser, or kirsch, made from cherries; Poire Williams, made from pears; framboise, made from raspberries; fraise, made from strawberries; and slivovitz, made from plums. These are true brandies, distilled directly from fruits. Other fruit-flavored brandies may actually be liqueurs created from a variety of liquors. They are not necessarily inferior, they're just not made directly from a fruit or a grape wine.

B&B

1 ounce Bénédictine

1 ounce brandy

Pour the Bénédictine and the brandy into a brandy snifter.

Baby Doll

2 ounces cognac

1½ ounces Grand Marnier

Juice from ½ lemon

Sugar, for rimming

Combine the cognac, Grand Marnier, and lemon juice in a shaker with ice. Shake well. Strain into a sugar-rimmed cocktail glass.

Angel's Share

"Angel's share" is a winemaking term for the portion of cognac that is lost to evaporation. Legend says that when you visit the Cognac region of France you can actually smell the cognac in the air.

Between the Sheets

¾ ounce light rum

¾ ounce brandy

¾ ounce triple sec

½ ounce lemon juice

1 lemon twist, for garnish

Combine the liquid ingredients in a shaker with ice. Shake well. Strain into a cocktail glass and garnish with lemon twist.

Bombay Cocktail

1 ounce brandy

½ ounce dry vermouth

½ ounce triple sec

½ ounce sweet vermouth

1 lemon twist, for garnish

Combine the liquid ingredients in a shaker nearly filled with ice. Shake well. Strain into a cocktail glass. Garnish with lemon twist.

Brandy Manhattan

1½ ounces brandy

1 ounce sweet vermouth

1 teaspoon sugar

Dash bitters

Combine the ingredients in a shaker of ice. Shake well. Strain into a cocktail glass.

Liquid Beauty

Some homemade shampoo and conditioner recipes call for common alcohols such as gin, rum, and vodka. If you look at the ingredients in your current shampoo and conditioner, you'll almost certainly find alcohol—although not the kind you'd ever want to drink!

Napoleon and Cognac

Napoleon loved cognac. As a matter of fact, he made the Courvoisier distillery his headquarters during the French Revolution. Today, Courvoisier makes a Napoleon cognac as a tribute.

Brandy Vermouth Classic

2 ounces brandy

½ ounce sweet vermouth

Dash bitters

Combine the ingredients in a mixing glass half filled with ice and stir. Strain into a cocktail glass.

Dirty Mother

1 ounce brandy

1 ounce coffee liqueur

Build the ingredients in an old-fashioned glass of ice.

Fancy Brandy

2 ounces brandy

¼ ounce Cointreau

¼ teaspoon sugar

Dash bitters

1 lemon twist, for garnish

Pour the liquid ingredients into a mixing glass nearly filled with ice and stir. Strain into a cocktail glass. Serve with a lemon twist.

Sniffing Cognac

The experts say that sniffing cognac is done in three stages: held at your chest, then at your neck, and finally at your nose. When sniffing, a wine glass works better than a snifter.

Keoke Coffee (Coffee Nudge)

½ ounce brandy

½ ounce coffee liqueur

Hot black coffee to fill

Pour the ingredients into an Irish coffee mug.

Sidecar

2 ounces brandy

½ ounce Cointreau

1 ounce fresh lemon juice

Combine the ingredients in a shaker nearly filled with ice. Shake well. Strain into a cocktail glass.

06. Aperitifs and Digestifs

*A*n aperitif (uh-pair-a-TEEF) is an alcoholic drink taken before dinner. Aperitifs are meant to stimulate your appetite. Leisurely get-togethers allow guests to savor their conversation and their drinks while they wait for their meal. Aperitifs include sherry, port, vermouths, and cocktails made with liqueurs like Campari, pastis, and sambuca. Although the first three mentioned are wine-based, they are not noted in the wine cocktails chapter because they are more pertinent to this chapter.

Cordials and liqueurs are often used as after-dinner drinks to aid digestion—thus, the name digestif. Europeans drink shots of limoncello, minted schnapps, grappa, and anise liqueurs. Today, after-dinner drinks tend to be either creamy, hot, or a neat measure of spirit. Nightcaps can be a hot drink or a single spirit that is sipped to make you feel warm and cozy inside.

Many liqueurs are quite sweet and can be served on their own as after-dinner drinks. The crèmes, whose creamy consistency stems from high sugar content, are the richest of all. The sweetness of a liqueur never overwhelms its fruit or herb character, and all add intense, distinctive flavors to mixed drinks.

For your bar cart, you will want to select a choice few of these spirits to keep on hand. If you like the taste of anise/licorice (pastis), there are many other choices for you—Galliano, anisette, ouzo, sambuca, pastis, Ricard, Pernod, or absinthe. Try using them interchangeably in the recipes in this chapter to see what you like best. Then tailor your cart to include a limited selection of options.

FLAVORS OF LIQUEURS

You can find many different kinds of liqueurs in a wide variety of flavors, from plum to banana! Below is a list of just a few, and their flavors.

ABSINTHE = anise/licorice

ADVOCAAT = eggnog

AMARETTO = almond

ANISETTE = anise/licorice

AQUAVIT = caraway

BAILEYS IRISH CREAM = vanilla, chocolate, and Irish whiskey

BÄRENJÄGER = honey

BÉNÉDICTINE = herbs and spices

BLUE CURAÇAO = orange

CHAMBORD = black raspberry

CHARTREUSE = herbs and spices

CHERRY HEERING = cherry

COFFEE LIQUEUR = coffee

KAHLÚA = coffee

LICHIDO = litchi (or lychee)

LICOR 43 = citrus vanilla

LIMONCELLO = sweet lemon

MALIBU = coconut

MANZANA = apple

MIDORI = honeydew melon

PARFAIT AMOUR = violets, rose, vanilla, and spice

PASSOÃ = passion fruit

PATXARAN = sloe berry, coffee bean, and vanilla

PERNOD = anise/licorice

PISANG AMBON = banana

PRUNELLE = plum

RAZZMATAZZ = raspberry

RUMPLE MINZE = peppermint

SAMBUCA = anise/ licorice

SLOE GIN = sloe berry

SOUTHERN COMFORT = peach, apricot, and honey

STREGA = herbs, mint, fennel, and saffron

TEQUILA ROSE = strawberry cream

TIA MARIA = coffee

TRIPLE SEC = orange

TSIPOURO = anise/licorice

TUACA = caramel, vanilla, orange

WHIDBEYS = loganberry

XTABENTUN = anise/licorice, honey

YUKON JACK = honey

Liqueurs add flavor to a polished drink, or they can be tasty on their own. Try them solo, or mix and match to see what tastes the best!

After Five

1 ounce Irish cream liqueur

1 ounce Kahlúa

1 ounce peppermint schnapps

Pour all ingredients into an ice-filled old-fashioned glass. Stir gently.

Americano

1 ounce Campari

1 ounce sweet vermouth

Pour the Campari and sweet vermouth into an old-fashioned glass filled with ice and stir.

The Americano

It's said that the Americano was created by Italian Gaspare Campari at his bar, Café Campari, in the 1860s. It originally had another name, but Gaspare noticed that the American tourists loved the drink so he renamed it.

Bittersweet Cocktail

1 ounce sweet vermouth

1 ounce dry vermouth

1 lemon twist

Pour the liquid ingredients into a mixing glass nearly filled with ice and stir. Strain into a cocktail glass. Add a lemon twist.

Black Honey

1½ ounces Drambuie

Hot coffee to fill

1 tablespoon honey

Whipped cream (optional)

Pour the Drambuie into an Irish coffee mug and fill with coffee. Add the honey and stir to dissolve. Top with whipped cream if you desire.

Black Russian

1 ounce Kahlúa

1 ounce vodka

Build in an old-fashioned glass of ice.

Colorado Bulldog

1 ounce coffee liqueur

1 ounce vodka

2 ounces cream

Cola to fill

Combine the coffee liqueur, vodka, and cream in a shaker. Shake well. Pour into a highball glass of ice and fill with cola.

Liqueur Brands

There are many liqueur brands on the market, but the top four that make crèmes, schnapps, cordials, and liqueurs are DeKuyper, Bols, Marie Brizard, and Hiram Walker.

Coronation

3 ounces dry sherry

½ ounce dry vermouth

Dash bitters

1 lemon twist, for garnish

Combine the liquid ingredients in a shaker half filled with ice. Shake well. Strain into a cocktail glass and garnish with lemon twist.

Cortés

1 ounce Kahlúa

1 ounce light rum

Dash lemon juice

Combine all ingredients and serve over cracked ice in a brandy snifter.

Crimson and Clover

2 ounces Southern Comfort

5 ounces cranberry juice

Sprinkle of ground cloves

Combine the ingredients in a shaker with ice. Shake well. Strain into an old-fashioned glass of ice.

Diablo Cocktail

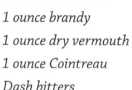

1 ounce brandy

1 ounce dry vermouth

1 ounce Cointreau

Dash bitters

Combine the ingredients in a shaker half filled with ice. Shake well. Strain into a cocktail glass.

Dry Negroni

1 ounce Campari

1 ounce gin

1 ounce dry vermouth

Pour the ingredients into an old-fashioned glass over ice. Stir gently.

Foreign Affair

2 ounces sambuca

1 ounce brandy

Combine both ingredients in a shaker with ice. Shake well. Strain into a cocktail glass.

Sambuca and Coffee Beans

Sambuca gets three coffee beans when served to savor. You can leave them out if you are serving it for shots. The beans are good luck and mean many things to many people. The most popular meanings are health, happiness, and prosperity.

Fuzzy Navel

2 ounces peach schnapps

Orange juice to fill

Pour the peach schnapps into a highball glass of ice and fill to the top with orange juice.

Godfather

1 ounce amaretto

1 ounce Scotch whisky

Pour the amaretto and Scotch into an old-fashioned glass with ice. Stir gently.

Godmother

1 ounce amaretto

1 ounce vodka

Pour the amaretto and vodka into an old-fashioned glass with ice. Stir gently.

Kahlúa and Cream

2 ounces Kahlúa

2 ounces cream

Build in an old-fashioned glass of ice. Serve layered.

Orgasm

1 ounce coffee liqueur

1 ounce amaretto

2 ounces Irish cream (optional)

2 ounces cream (optional)

Combine the ingredients in a shaker. Shake well. Pour into an old-fashioned glass of ice. Irish cream and regular cream can be added if desired.

Peppermint Pattie

1 ounce dark crème de cacao

1 ounce white crème de menthe

2 ounces cream (optional)

Pour the ingredients into an old-fashioned glass of ice. Cream can be added if desired.

Platinum Blonde Coffee

1½ ounces Godiva White Chocolate Liqueur

Hot black coffee to fill

Whipped cream, for garnish (optional)

Pour the Godiva liqueur into an Irish coffee mug and fill with coffee. Garnish with whipped cream if desired.

Queen Elizabeth

1 ounce Bénédictine

2 ounces sweet vermouth

Combine both ingredients in a shaker with ice. Shake well. Strain into a cocktail glass.

Scarlett O'Hara

2 ounces Southern Comfort

3 ounces cranberry juice

Build in an old-fashioned glass of ice and stir.

Smith and Kearns

2 ounces coffee liqueur

2 ounces cream

Club soda to fill

Combine the coffee liqueur and cream in a shaker. Shake well. Pour into a highball glass of ice. Top with club soda.

Smith and Wesson

1 ounce coffee liqueur

1 ounce vodka

2 ounces half-and-half

Club soda to fill

Pour the first three ingredients into a highball glass of ice. Top with club soda.

Southern Hospitality

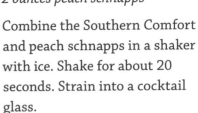

2 ounces Southern Comfort

2 ounces peach schnapps

Combine the Southern Comfort and peach schnapps in a shaker with ice. Shake for about 20 seconds. Strain into a cocktail glass.

Toasted Almond

1 ounce coffee liqueur

1 ounce amaretto

2 ounces cream

Combine the ingredients in a shaker. Shake well. Pour into an old-fashioned glass of ice.

Tootsie Roll

1 ounce coffee liqueur

1 ounce dark crème de cacao

3 ounces orange juice

Combine the ingredients in a shaker with ice. Shake well. Strain into a cocktail glass or pour over an old-fashioned glass of ice.

Crème versus Cream

A cream liqueur is not to be confused with a crème liqueur. If it says cream, it includes dairy cream. The best example is Baileys Irish Cream. Crèmes have a lot of sugar added, giving them a syrup-like consistency. Crème refers to the consistency. Examples are crème de cacao, crème de menthe, and crème de banana.

07. Vodka Cocktails

*M*ilk comes from cows, wool comes from sheep, and vodka comes from potatoes, right? Not so fast. Yes, some vodka is made from potatoes. But unlike many spirits, vodka can be made from practically anything that contains sugar or starch. Common ingredients (aside from potatoes, of course) include root vegetables like beets, and grains such as corn and rye.

Legend says that in the 1300s, Genoese merchants en route to Lithuania brought this water of life (*aqua vitae*) to Moscow. Other sources contend that vodka originated in Poland and Russia without any assistance from the Genoese. Regardless, by the 1700s people were infusing vodka with herb and fruit flavors like sage, cherry, dill, blackberry, and caraway. (And we thought our modern society created flavored vodka!) Vodka didn't make it into American liquor cabinets until the 1930s—and the brand was Smirnoff. The classic cocktail Moscow Mule became popular in the 1950s despite its association with the menacing Communists on the other side of the Iron Curtain. In 1962, the first James Bond film showed 007 ordering a Martini made with Smirnoff, and vodka skyrocketed straight to the top. It has remained the number-one spirit in America since.

Vodka is a profound silent partner. Because it is chameleon-like, taking on the tastes of anything around it, flavored versions have flourished. Since the turn of the twenty-first century a constant production of new high-end vodkas has appeared, each with its own little gimmick—vodka made with ice harvested from icebergs, black-colored vodka, vodka filtered multiple times, vodka infused with rose petals, vodka distilled from organic grains . . . the list goes on. But you don't have to keep fifteen flavors of vodka around to satisfy your guests. That's not the bar cart way! Pick one good brand that you like and let the mixers and other ingredients define the flavor.

Arctic Circle

1 ounce vodka

½ ounce lime juice

Ginger ale to fill

Crushed mint leaves, for garnish (optional)

Pour the vodka and lime juice into an ice-filled highball glass. Add ginger ale. Garnish with crushed mint leaves, if desired.

Cutting Tools

A serrated knife is the best knife to use when cutting garnishes, and a cutting board that is not used for cutting meat is preferred. As a safety precaution, place a wet bar towel under the cutting board to avoid slippage.

Baybreeze

1½ ounces vodka

Equal parts of cranberry and pineapple juice to fill

Pour all ingredients into a highball glass of ice.

Black Goose

1 ounce vodka, preferably Grey Goose

1 ounce coffee liqueur

Pour both ingredients into an old-fashioned glass of ice and stir.

Bling Bling

2 ounces vodka

2 ounces white grape juice

1 ounce 7Up

Pour all ingredients over ice into a highball glass. Stir gently.

Bloody Caesar

1½ shots vodka

¼ shot fresh lime juice

Clamato juice to fill

*Celery salt, pepper, Tabasco sauce,
Worcestershire sauce, to taste*

Celery stalk, for garnish (optional)

Combine all liquid ingredients
and spices with ice and stir.
Strain into a highball glass filled
with ice. Garnish with celery
stalk, if desired.

Bloody Mary

2 ounces vodka

Bloody Mary mix to fill

*Celery stalk and lime wedge, for
garnish (optional)*

Combine the vodka and Bloody
Mary mix; stir with ice. Strain
into a highball glass filled with
ice. Garnish with celery stalk and
lime wedge, if desired.

Bloody Mary History

Tomato juice followed quickly
on the heels of the juicer,
which was introduced in 1921.
The Bloody Mary, a simple
concoction of vodka and
tomato juice, has disputed ori-
gins. Bartender Fernand Pet-
iot claimed to have invented
the drink in the late 1920s
in Paris. Another contender,
George Jessel, said he mixed
the drink for himself to cure a
hangover. It is unknown who
the Bloody Mary's namesake
was, but the drink was not
named for the Catholic Tudor
queen who earned the grisly
nickname after ordering Prot-
estant purges.

Caipiroska

½ lime

2 teaspoons sugar

2 ounces vodka

Muddle the lime and sugar in a mixing glass. Add the vodka and ice. Shake, then strain into an old-fashioned glass of cracked ice.

Candy Apple

2 ounces vodka

5 ounces 7Up

1 ounce lime juice

Splash grenadine

Pour the ingredients into a highball glass over ice. Stir.

The Cape Codder

The Cape Codder gets its name from the mixer used—cranberry juice. It refers to the cranberries that grow in and around Cape Cod in Massachusetts. In the fall, the berries turn a bright red color.

Cape Codder

1 ounce vodka

Cranberry juice to fill

1 lime wedge, for garnish (optional)

Fill a highball glass with ice. Add the vodka. Fill with cranberry juice. Garnish with lime wedge if desired.

Cedarwood

2 ounces vodka

4 ounces cranberry juice

1 ounce lemon juice

3 ounces ginger ale

Pour the ingredients into a highball glass over ice. Stir.

Chi-Chi

1½ ounces vodka

4 ounces Piña Colada mix

1 pineapple slice and 1 cherry, for garnish (optional)

Pour the liquid ingredients into a blender with a cup of ice. Blend. Pour into a highball glass. Garnish with pineapple slice and cherry, if desired.

Chocolate Martini

2 ounces vodka

½ ounce crème de cacao

1 chocolate chip or Hershey's Kisses piece, for garnish (optional)

Cocoa powder, for rimming (optional)

Combine the liquid ingredients in a shaker with ice. Shake vigorously. Strain into a chilled cocktail glass. Garnish with a chocolate chip, or coat the rim of the glass with cocoa powder.

Comfortable, Fuzzy Screw

1½ ounces vodka

1½ ounces Southern Comfort

1½ ounces peach schnapps

Orange juice to fill

Pour the first three ingredients into a highball glass over ice. Add orange juice to fill.

Cosmopolitan

1 ounce vodka

½ ounce triple sec or Cointreau

½ ounce cranberry juice

¼ ounce lime juice

Combine the ingredients in a shaker half filled with ice. Shake well. Strain into a cocktail glass. Flavored vodkas can be used to vary the taste.

Dirty Girl Scout Cookie

1 ounce vodka

1 ounce coffee liqueur

1 ounce Irish cream liqueur

¼ ounce green crème de menthe

Combine the ingredients in a shaker half filled with ice. Shake well. Strain into an old-fashioned glass with ice.

Salty Snacks

Back in saloon times, proprietors offered free lunches. Most were overly salted, which encouraged the thirsty diner to buy an alcoholic drink. Many bars now offer peanuts and salty snacks for the same reason.

Dirty Vodka Martini

3 ounces vodka

1 ounce dry vermouth

½ ounce olive brine

Olive, for garnish

Combine the vodka and vermouth in a shaker with ice and stir. Slowly add the olive brine. (Too much brine can ruin this drink so proceed with caution.) Stir again. Strain into a cocktail glass. Garnish with olive. May be shaken instead of stirred.

Fumble

1 ounce vodka

1 ounce gin

1 ounce grapefruit juice

1 ounce cranberry juice

Club soda or seltzer to fill

Combine the vodka, gin, and both juices in a shaker half filled with ice. Shake well. Strain into an old-fashioned glass packed with ice. Add soda to fill.

Gypsy

1 ounce vodka

½ ounce Bénédictine

Dash bitters

Combine the ingredients in a shaker with ice. Shake well. Strain into a cocktail glass.

Hairy Navel

1 ounce vodka

1½ ounces peach schnapps

Orange juice to fill

Pour the vodka and schnapps into a highball glass over all. Add orange juice to fill. Stir.

Jericho's Breeze

1 ounce vodka

¾ ounce blue curaçao

2½ ounces sweet-and-sour mix

Splash lemon-lime soda

Splash orange juice

Pineapple spear and cherry, for garnish (optional)

Combine the liquid ingredients in a shaker with ice. Shake until frothy. Strain into a white wine glass. Garnish with pineapple spear and cherry, if desired.

Kamikaze

1½ ounces vodka

1 ounce lime juice

1 ounce triple sec

1 lime wedge, for garnish

Combine the liquid ingredients in a shaker with ice. Shake well. Strain into a cocktail glass. Garnish with the lime wedge.

Laughing at the Waves

1½ ounces vodka

½ ounce dry vermouth

½ ounce Campari

Combine the ingredients in a shaker with ice. Stir well. Strain into cocktail glass.

Lemon Drop

1½ ounces vodka

¾ ounce lemon juice

1 teaspoon simple syrup

1 lemon twist, for garnish

Combine the liquid ingredients in a shaker with ice. Shake well. Strain into a chilled cocktail glass. Garnish with the lemon twist.

Madras

1½ ounces vodka

Equal parts of orange and cranberry juice to fill

Pour the vodka into a highball glass of ice. Fill with the juices. Stir.

Moscow Mule

2 ounces vodka (Smirnoff, if you want to be truly authentic)

1 ounce fresh lime juice

Ginger beer to fill

Pour the ingredients into a highball glass nearly filled with ice. Stir well.

Frozen Mudslide

The Mudslide drink can be made frozen but that requires a blender. If making frozen, pour the Mudslide ingredients into a blender with a cup of ice. Blend, then pour into a tall chocolate-swirled glass and top off with whipped cream.

Mudslide

1 ounce vodka

½ ounce coffee liqueur

½ ounce Irish cream

Half-and-half to fill

Chocolate syrup, for garnish (optional)

Pour the vodka, coffee liqueur, Irish cream, and half-and-half into an old-fashioned glass of ice. Pour into a shaker. Shake and pour back into the glass and serve. Garnish with chocolate syrup, if desired.

Screwdriver

1½ ounces vodka

2½ ounces freshly squeezed orange juice

Fill an old-fashioned glass with ice. Add the ingredients and stir.

Seabreeze

1½ ounces vodka

Cranberry and grapefruit juice to fill

1 lime wedge, for garnish

Pour the liquid ingredients into a highball glass over ice. Garnish with lime wedge.

Vodka Collins

2 ounces vodka

1 ounce fresh lemon juice

¼ ounce simple syrup

Club soda to fill

1 orange slice and 1 cherry, for garnish (optional)

Shake the first three ingredients with ice. Strain into a highball glass. Fill with club soda and garnish with orange slice and cherry, if desired.

Wet Your Whistle

One explanation for the origin of this phrase is that English pubs used to have cups with whistles built into them. A patron in need of a refill would use the whistle to get the barmaid's attention. However, you'd be hard-pressed to find any of these whistling vessels in London today—probably because they never existed in the first place. There is no archaeological evidence of these cups.

Vodka Gimlet

2 ounces vodka

½ ounce Rose's lime juice (or ¼ ounce fresh lime juice and ¼ ounce simple syrup)

1 lime wedge, for garnish

Add the liquid ingredients to a mixing glass half filled with ice. Shake and strain into an old-fashioned glass of ice. Garnish with lime wedge.

Vodka Martini

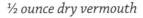

½ ounce dry vermouth

2 ounces vodka

2 olives or 1 lemon twist, for garnish

In a mixing glass half filled with ice, add the vermouth first, then the vodka. Stir, then strain into a cocktail glass. Serve with olives or a twist of lemon.

Vodka Red Bull

2 ounces vodka

Red Bull to fill

Pour the vodka into a highball glass of ice. Fill with Red Bull.

Vodka Sour

2 ounces vodka

1 ounce fresh lemon juice

¼ ounce simple syrup

1 orange slice and 1 cherry, for garnish (optional)

Fill a shaker glass two-thirds with ice. Add liquid ingredients and shake. Strain into a highball glass of ice. Garnish with orange slice and cherry, if desired.

White Russian

1 ounce vodka

1 ounce coffee liqueur

2 ounces cream

Combine the ingredients in a shaker. Shake well. Strain into an old-fashioned glass of ice.

Woo Woo

1 ounce vodka

1 ounce peach schnapps

Cranberry juice to fill

Pour the vodka and peach schnapps into a highball glass. Fill with cranberry juice.

08. Gin Cocktails

*I*n its basic form, gin is vodka that has been redistilled with herbs and botanicals. Gin makers use citrus peels, coriander, ginger, rose petals, nutmeg, and cassia bark, but the most prominent is the juniper berry.

The four main categories of gin are:

- **GENEVER** (also spelled jenever)
- **LONDON DRY GIN**
- **PLYMOUTH ENGLISH GIN**
- **NEW WESTERN**

The word *genever* is Dutch for juniper, and the word *gin* is a shortening of the Dutch term. Holland and Belgium make genever, which is considered the original style of gin made in pot stills. It's sweeter than London dry gin. London dry gin is the most popular because it mixes well. It doesn't have to be made in England (the United States, Germany, and Spain make gin as well). Plymouth English gin can only be made in Plymouth, England—and it was the first gin used in a printed recipe of the Martini. The New Western gins use less juniper and more ingredients like rose petals and cucumber. Examples of these are Hendrick's, Aviation, and Martin Miller's.

The key to a successful bar cart is in selecting the right ingredients for you and your guests. So, you don't need to keep four different kinds of gin on hand. Select a type and brand that you like best—the research is the fun part!—and keep that on hand. Tailor your recipe collection to include those drinks that work best with that gin. Remember that the bar cart is about curating, and a good curator doesn't try to have a lot of everything. A good curator picks the best of the best.

Apple Ginger Gin

2 ounces gin, preferably London dry

2 ounces apple juice

Ginger beer to fill

Pour the gin and apple juice into a large cocktail glass. Fill with ginger beer. Stir.

> **Gin Inventor?**
> Dr. Franciscus Sylvius, a Dutch professor and physician, is credited with making gin as a cure-all tonic in the 1650s. Today, many alcohol historians dispute this claim because the juniper berry was quite plentiful in Italy, which leads them to believe that Italian monks were the first to make gin.

Bee's Knees

2 ounces gin

¾ ounce honey

½ ounce fresh lemon juice

Combine the ingredients in a shaker with ice. Shake well. Strain into a cocktail glass.

Bronx

1 ounce dry gin

1 ounce French dry vermouth

1 ounce fresh orange juice

Combine the ingredients in a shaker with ice. Shake well. Strain into a cocktail glass.

Bull Dog

1½ ounces gin

2 ounces fresh orange juice

Ginger ale to fill

Pour the gin and orange juice into a highball glass with ice. Fill with ginger ale. Stir.

Kitty Cat Gin

Old Tom Gin is the only produced example we have today of what sweetened gin used to taste like. This gin got its name from a cat-shaped plaque that was mounted on the outside of some English pubs in the eighteenth century. One could deposit money in the cat's mouth and then place their mouth on a tube between the cats paws. A barman inside would pour a dram of gin into the tube. How about that for a vending machine!

Cash Out

1 ounce gin

½ ounce Grand Marnier

Orange twist, for garnish (optional)

Combine the liquid ingredients in a shaker with ice. Stir well. Strain into a cocktail glass and garnish with an orange twist, if desired.

Cotton Gin

2 ounces London dry gin

1 ounce sambuca

Combine ingredients in a shaker with ice. Shake well. Strain into a cocktail glass. The water from the ice will turn this drink white.

Cowboy Martini

3 ounces Plymouth gin

¼ ounce simple syrup

2 dashes orange bitters

4 or 5 mint leaves (partially torn)

1 orange twist, for garnish (optional)

Combine the liquid ingredients and the mint in a shaker with ice. Shake well. Strain into a cocktail glass. Garnish with orange twist, if desired.

Dirty Martini

2 ounces London dry gin
½ ounce olive juice
Olives, for garnish

Combine the liquid ingredients in a shaker with ice. Shake well. Strain into a cocktail glass. Garnish with olives.

Dragonfly

1½ ounces gin
4 ounces ginger ale
1 lime wedge, for garnish

Pour the liquid ingredients into a highball glass almost filled with ice. Stir well. Garnish with lime wedge.

Dutch Trade Winds

2 ounces gin (preferably genever)
½ ounce curaçao
½ ounce lemon juice
1 teaspoon simple syrup

Combine the ingredients in a shaker half filled with ice. Shake well. Strain into a cocktail glass.

Gibson

1½ ounces dry gin
½ ounce French vermouth
3 pearl onions, for garnish
1 lemon twist, for garnish

Combine the gin and vermouth in a shaker with ice. Shake well. Strain into a cocktail glass. Garnish with onions and a lemon twist.

Gimlet

2 ounces gin

¾ ounce sweetened lime juice (or fresh lime juice and simple syrup)

1 lime wedge, for garnish

Shake the gin and lime juice in a shaker of ice. Strain into an old-fashioned glass of ice. Garnish with lime wedge.

Gin and It

2 ounces gin

¾ ounce sweet vermouth

Pour the ingredients into a mixing glass of ice and stir. Strain into a cocktail glass.

Gin and Juice

1½ ounces gin

Orange juice to fill

Pour the gin into a highball glass of ice. Fill with orange juice. Stir.

Gin and Sin

2 ounces gin

¼ ounce lemon juice

¼ ounce orange juice

¼ ounce grenadine

Combine the ingredients in a shaker with ice. Shake well. Strain into a cocktail glass.

Gin and Tonic

1½ ounces gin

Tonic to fill

1 lime wedge, for garnish

Pour the gin into a highball glass of ice. Fill with tonic. Garnish with lime wedge.

Gin Cobbler

2 ounces club soda

1 teaspoon fine sugar

1 ounce gin

1 lemon or lime slice, for garnish

Pour the club soda into a large white wine glass. Add the sugar and dissolve. Fill with crushed ice. Add the gin and stir. Garnish with lemon or lime slice. Serve with a straw, if desired.

Gin Daisy

2 ounces gin

¼ ounce Grand Marnier

¼ ounce simple syrup

Juice from ½ lemon

Club soda to fill

Combine the first four ingredients in a shaker with ice. Shake well. Strain into a large white wine glass. Fill with club soda.

Gin-Gin Mule

1½ ounces gin

¾ ounce lime juice

1 ounce simple syrup

6 sprigs mint

1 ounce ginger beer

Combine the first four ingredients in a shaker with of ice. Shake well. Strain into a highball glass of ice. Top with ginger beer.

Gin Rickey

2 ounces gin

Juice from 1 lime

Club soda to fill

Shake the gin and lime juice in a shaker of ice. Strain into a highball glass of ice. Fill with club soda.

Gin Sour

2 ounces gin

1 ounce lemon juice

1 teaspoon fine sugar (or 1½ ounces sweet-and-sour mix instead of lemon and sugar)

Combine the ingredients in a shaker with ice. Shake well. Strain into a cocktail glass.

Hawaiian Cocktail

2 ounces gin

½ ounce triple sec

½ ounce pineapple juice

Combine the ingredients in a shaker with ice. Shake well. Strain into a cocktail glass.

Jasmine

1½ ounces gin

¼ ounce Cointreau

¾ ounce lemon juice

¼ ounce Campari

Combine the ingredients in a shaker with ice. Shake well. Strain into a cocktail glass.

Magnolia Blossom

1½ ounces gin

½ ounce cream

½ ounce fresh lemon juice

¼ ounce grenadine

Combine the ingredients in a shaker with ice. Shake well. Strain into a chilled cocktail glass.

Martini

2 ounces gin

⅛ ounce dry vermouth

2 large pimiento-stuffed green olives

Shake gin and vermouth in a shaker of ice. Strain into a cocktail glass. Garnish with the olives.

Misting the Vermouth
Some people pour the dry vermouth into a mister and mist the top of the Martini.

King of Cocktails
The Martini is the king of cocktails. It is the icon of the cocktail culture and whole books have been written about its simplicity—with a dash of controversy. You should know that no one knows when, where, or by whom the first Martini was created. What we do know is that Jerry Thomas published a cocktail recipe called a Martinez in his *Bar-Tenders Guide* in 1887.

Million-Dollar Cocktail

1½ ounces gin

1 ounce sweet vermouth

1½ ounces pineapple juice

½ ounce lemon juice

1 ounce cream

¼ ounce simple syrup

¼ ounce grenadine

Combine the ingredients in a shaker with ice. Shake well. Strain into a cocktail glass.

Monkey Gland

2 ounces gin

1 ounce orange juice

Dash Pernod

¼ ounce grenadine

1 orange twist, for garnish

Combine the liquid ingredients in a shaker with ice. Shake well. Strain into a cocktail glass. Garnish with orange twist.

NASCAR Beginnings

During Prohibition, bootleggers carrying moonshine would soup up their car engines in order to outrun the police. After Prohibition, they raced each other on country roads for the fun of it. These were the humble offshoot beginnings of NASCAR. A legendary moonshiner of the 1940s and 1950s named Junior Johnson was one of NASCAR's first drivers.

Negroni

1 ounce gin

1 ounce sweet vermouth

1 ounce Campari

1 orange twist, for garnish (optional)

Combine the liquid ingredients in a shaker with ice. Shake well. Strain into an old-fashioned glass of ice. Garnish with orange twist, if desired.

Ninja Turtle

1 ounce gin

½ ounce blue curaçao

Fresh orange juice to fill

Pour the gin and curaçao into a highball glass of ice. Fill with orange juice.

Park Avenue

1½ ounces gin

¼ ounce dry vermouth

¼ ounce sweet vermouth

¼ ounce pineapple juice

Combine the ingredients in a shaker with ice. Shake well. Strain into a chilled cocktail glass.

Pegu Club

2 ounces dry gin

1 ounce curaçao

¼ ounce lime juice

Dash Angostura bitters

Dash orange bitters

Combine the ingredients in a shaker with ice. Shake well. Strain into a cocktail glass.

Pink Gin

2–3 ounces gin

3 or 4 dashes Angostura bitters

Combine the ingredients in a shaker with ice. Shake well. Strain into a cocktail glass.

The Pegu Club

The original Pegu Club entertained British colonial officers stationed in Burma. It was renowned for its cocktails, and its house drink gained worldwide popularity by the 1930s. The club has closed, but master bartender Audrey Saunders has introduced a Pegu Club in New York City. The new Pegu Club strives to make cocktails the way they were supposed to be made, with fresh ingredients and a commitment to superior mixology.

Rusty Windmill

1 ounce gin (preferably genever)

1 ounce Drambuie

Pour the ingredients into an old-fashioned glass of ice.

Tom Collins

1½ ounces gin

2 ounces sweet-and-sour mix

Club soda or Sprite to fill

Fill a highball glass, also known as a Collins glass, with ice. Add the gin, sweet-and-sour mix, and the club soda or Sprite. Stir vigorously to work up a bit of a froth.

White Lady

1½ ounces gin (preferably Plymouth)

¾ ounce Cointreau

¾ ounce fresh lemon juice

1 lemon twist, for garnish

Combine the liquid ingredients in a shaker with ice. Shake well. Strain into a cocktail glass. Garnish with lemon twist.

09. Rum Cocktails

*R*um is a spirit distilled from sugar cane and its by-products—sugar cane juice or molasses. It's produced in hot climates. It comes in three styles: white (light), gold (aged), and dark.

Beginning in the 1600s, members of the British Royal Navy received a half pint of rum a day to ward off scurvy. Alas, it didn't work (scurvy is caused by a vitamin C deficiency). Nonetheless, Britannia ruled the oceans for many years. The rum the British sailors drank was a crude alcohol that bears little resemblance to the spirit we enjoy today. We owe the transformation to a family by the name of Bacardí. In the 1800s, a Spanish wine merchant named Don Facundo Bacardí Massó moved with his family to Cuba. He and his brother José opened a small store and developed a passion for making rum. They were determined to create the first smooth rum. The result was Bacardi rum, and today it's the most popular rum in the world.

As with vodka, there are different flavors of rum—spiced rum, coconut rum—but except for those times when you're showcasing a special drink or throwing a themed party, choose your favorite unflavored rum to keep on your bar cart. Or, if you and your friends particularly like rum drinks, keep one light and one dark on hand.

Acapulco

1¾ ounces rum

½ ounce triple sec

½ ounce lime juice

1 teaspoon sugar

Combine the ingredients in a shaker with ice. Shake well. Strain into a cocktail glass.

The Real McCoy

In rum-running times, captains would add water to the rum bottles to stretch their profits. Captain William "Bill" McCoy was one captain who did not cut his rum, and one theory states that's where we get the phrase "the real McCoy."

Adam

2 ounces dark rum

1 ounce lemon juice

1 teaspoon grenadine

Combine the ingredients in a shaker with ice. Shake well. Strain into a cocktail glass.

Bacardi Cocktail

1½ ounces Bacardi light rum

¾ ounce lemon juice

1 ounce simple syrup

2 dashes grenadine

Combine the ingredients in a shaker with ice. Shake well. Strain into a cocktail glass.

Barely Legal

1 ounce Amaretto

1 ounce 151 rum

Dr. Pepper or Pibb Xtra to fill

Pour the Amaretto and rum into a highball glass over ice. Add soda to fill. Stir.

Bat Bite

1¼ ounces dark rum

4 ounces cranberry juice

1 lime wedge, for garnish

Pour the ingredients into a highball glass with ice. Garnish with wedge of lime.

Batiste

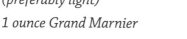

2 ounces rum (preferably light)

1 ounce Grand Marnier

Combine the ingredients in a shaker with ice. Shake well. Strain into a cocktail glass.

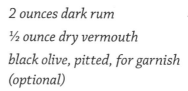

Mind Your Ps and Qs

We get the phrase "mind your Ps and Qs" from old English pubs. In old England, patrons ordered ale in pints and quarts. When they got unruly, the bartender would yell at them to mind their own pints and quarts and settle down.

Black Devil

2 ounces dark rum

½ ounce dry vermouth

black olive, pitted, for garnish (optional)

Combine the ingredients in a shaker with ice. Stir well. Strain into a cocktail glass. Garnish with pitted black olive, if desired.

Blue Hawaiian

*1 ounce rum
(preferably light)*

1 ounce blue curaçao

Pineapple juice to fill

*1 pineapple slice, for garnish
(optional)*

Pour the liquid ingredients into a highball glass of ice. Stir. Garnish with pineapple slice, if desired.

Bolo

*2 ounces rum
(preferably light)*

1 ounce lime juice

1 ounce orange juice

1 teaspoon fine sugar

Combine the ingredients in a shaker nearly filled with ice. Shake well. Strain into a cocktail glass.

Boston Cooler

1 ounce lemon juice

1 teaspoon fine sugar

3 ounces club soda or ginger ale

2 ounces rum

1 lemon twist, for garnish

Into a highball glass, pour the lemon juice, sugar, and a bit of soda. Stir. Nearly fill glass with ice. Add rum and remaining soda and stir. Garnish with lemon twist.

Boston Sidecar

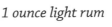

1 ounce light rum

½ ounce brandy

¾ ounce triple sec

1 ounce lime juice

Combine the ingredients in a shaker with ice. Shake well. Strain into a cocktail glass.

Bushwacker

*2 ounces rum
(preferably dark)*

1 ounce coffee liqueur

4 ounces Piña Colada mix

Blend all ingredients in a blender with 1 cup of ice. Pour into a highball glass.

Captain's Blood

1½ ounces dark rum

¼ ounce lime juice

¼ ounce simple syrup

2 dashes bitters

1 lemon peel spiral, for garnish

Combine the ingredients in a shaker with ice. Shake well. Strain into a cocktail glass. Garnish with spiral of lemon peel.

Caribbean Eclipse

2 ounces rum

1 ounce dark crème de cacao

1 ounce fresh lime juice

½ ounce simple syrup

Combine the ingredients in a shaker with ice. Shake well. Strain into a cocktail glass.

Cuba Libre (Rum and Coke)

2 lime wedges

2 ounces Cuban rum

Coke to fill

Fill a highball glass with ice. Squeeze the juice of one of the lime wedges over the ice and discard the wedge. Pour in the rum and fill with cola. Squeeze the second lime wedge into the drink. Swipe the rim with the lime and drop it into the drink.

Cuban Martini

Sugar, for rimming (optional)

3 ounces light rum

½ ounce dry vermouth

1 lime twist, for garnish

Rim cocktail glass with sugar, if desired. Combine the liquid ingredients in a shaker with ice. Shake well. Strain into a cocktail glass. Garnish with lime twist.

Daiquiri

1½ ounces light rum

1 ounce simple syrup

¾ ounce fresh lime juice

Combine the ingredients in a shaker with ice. Shake well. Strain into a cocktail glass.

Dark 'n' Stormy

2 ounces rum

Ginger beer to fill

1 lime wedge

Pour the rum over ice in a highball glass and fill with ginger beer. Squeeze in the lime wedge.

Flamingo

1½ ounces light rum

1½ ounces pineapple juice

¼ ounce lime juice

¼ ounce grenadine

Combine the ingredients in a shaker with ice. Shake well. Strain into a cocktail glass.

Golden Friendship

1 ounce light rum

1 ounce sweet vermouth

1 ounce amaretto

4 ounces ginger ale

Cherry, for garnish (optional)

Pour the rum, vermouth, and amaretto in a highball glass of ice. Fill with ginger ale. Garnish with cherry, if desired.

Hurricane

1 ounce light rum

1 ounce dark rum

1 ounce passion fruit juice (optional)

Fruit punch to fill

1 orange slice and cherry, for garnish (optional)

Combine the liquid ingredients in a shaker with ice. Shake well. Strain into a highball glass or a hurricane glass of ice. Garnish with orange slice and cherry, if desired.

Pat O'Brien's

The most famous bar in New Orleans, Pat O'Brien's, invented the Hurricane. During World War II, whiskey was in low supply but there was plenty of rum. The hurricane glass is modeled after a hurricane lamp.

Jolly Roger

2 ounces light rum

2 ounces Drambuie

1 ounce lime juice

Club soda to fill

Combine the first three ingredients in a shaker with ice. Shake well. Strain into a highball glass of ice. Fill with club soda.

Maraschino Cherries

Only infuse alcohol with cherries that do not contain artificial flavorings or colorings. The bright red cherries in a jar are made by taking real cherries, pitting them, and bleaching them white. The cherries are then dyed with red color #40. Use fresh cherries or look for the jarred dark red cherries. Check the label for any artificial ingredients.

Little Bastard

1 ounce rum

1 ounce orange juice

½ ounce pineapple juice

7Up to fill

Combine the ingredients except 7Up in a shaker with ice. Shake well. Strain into a highball glass and fill with 7Up.

Mai Tai Me Up

1 ounce dark rum

½ ounce light rum

1 ounce pineapple juice

1 ounce lemon juice

½ ounce simple syrup

1 slice canned pineapple and 1 maraschino cherry, for garnish (optional)

Shake liquid ingredients in a cocktail shaker with ice. Strain into a cocktail glass. Garnish with pineapple and cherry, if desired.

Mojito

3 sprigs mint (reserve 1 for garnish)

Juice of ½ lime

2 teaspoons of sugar

1½ ounces light rum

Club soda to fill

Muddle 2 sprigs of mint, lime, and sugar in a mixing glass. Add the rum. Pour this mixture into a shaker with ice. Shake well. Strain into a highball glass of cracked ice. Fill with club soda and garnish with mint sprig.

007 Does It Again

In the film *Die Another Day* (2002), James Bond drinks Champagne Bollinger, Havana rum, two vodka Martinis (one with an olive), and a Mojito. The Mojito's popularity exploded soon after.

Peaches at the Beaches

2 ounces peach schnapps

1 ounce light rum

¼ ounce grenadine

Orange juice to fill

Paper parasol, for garnish (optional)

Pour the peach schnapps, light rum, and grenadine into a highball glass of ice. Fill with orange juice. Garnish with paper parasol, if desired.

Pineapple Fizz

2 ounces light rum

1 ounce pineapple juice

1 teaspoon fine sugar

Club soda to fill

1 lemon twist, for garnish

Combine the rum, juice, and sugar in a shaker with ice. Shake well. Strain into a highball glass over ice. Add the club soda to fill. Garnish with lemon twist.

Pink Daiquiri

3 ounces rum

1 ounce lime juice

½ ounce grenadine

Combine the ingredients in a shaker with ice. Shake vigorously. Pour without straining into a champagne glass.

Planter's Punch

2 ounces light rum

1 ounce dark rum

2 ounces orange juice

1 ounce each lime juice, lemon juice, and pineapple juice

1 dash triple sec

1 dash grenadine

Assorted fruit for garnish, such as slices of orange and pineapple, wedges of lemon and lime, a cherry (optional)

Combine the ingredients except the triple sec, grenadine, and fruit garnishes in a shaker half filled with ice. Shake well. Strain into a highball glass nearly filled with ice. Top with triple sec and grenadine. Garnish as desired.

Rum Diablo

2 ounces rum

½ ounce Cointreau

½ ounce dry vermouth

2 dashes bitters

Orange twist, for garnish (optional)

Combine the ingredients in a shaker with ice. Stir well. Strain into a cocktail glass. Garnish with an orange twist, if desired.

Scorpion

1 ounce light rum

1 ounce brandy

½ ounce amaretto

¾ ounce lemon juice

½ ounce simple syrup

1 ounce orange juice

1 pineapple slice and 1 cherry, for garnish (optional)

Combine all liquid ingredients in a shaker with ice. Shake well. Strain into a highball glass of ice. Garnish with pineapple slice and cherry, if desired.

Swinging Chad

2 ounces golden rum

2 ounces pineapple juice

2 dashes Angostura bitters

Dash absinthe

Ginger ale to fill

Fill a highball glass with ice and add the ingredients. Stir.

10. Tequila Cocktails

*T*equila is North America's first distilled spirit. The name comes from a Mexican town of the same name in the state of Jalisco. Tequila is made from the heart of the agave plant. Legend has it that the Aztec ruler Montezuma welcomed the Spanish explorer Hernando Cortés with a wine made from the agave plant. The ungrateful Cortés became Montezuma's conqueror, took the agave wine, and distilled it to make tequila. This all took place around the early 1500s. By the 1600s tequila was being mass-produced. Jose Cuervo tequila was officially introduced in 1795.

With its distinctive dry taste, tequila is the basis for marvelous drinks, not the least of which is the Margarita. There are five types of tequila:

- **BLANCO** (not aged, and also called white or silver)
- **JOVEN** (blanco that is colored to look gold)
- **REPOSADO** (gold from aging)
- **AÑEJO** (aged the longest in oak barrels where it acquires its mellow color of gold)
- **MADURO** (mature, vintage, or ultra aged)

Maduro tequilas were first introduced in 2006. This tequila is aged a minimum of 3 years in oak barrels from France and Canada. The result is a smooth, superior spirit that is often called the cognac of tequila.

The blanco tequilas are usually on the less expensive end of the spectrum while añejo and maduro tequilas are on the more expensive end. To select the best tequila for your bar cart, try mixing different brands into your favorite cocktails (Margaritas, anyone?) and see what you and your guests like best. You may be surprised to find that the blanco blends better than the reposado. Or you may decide you prefer to invest a little more in just one aged tequila. Either way, your bar cart is about choosing what's right for you.

Alamo Splash

1 ounce tequila

1 ounce orange juice

1 ounce pineapple juice

Sprite or 7Up to fill

Pour the first three ingredients into a highball glass of ice. Fill with Sprite or 7Up.

Liquor Law

By law, for a liquor to be called and labeled tequila, 51 percent of it must be made from the blue agave plant grown near the town of Tequila. The best tequilas are 100 percent agave. Tequilas made with less than 100 percent agave are called mixtos. While they are less expensive than 100 percent agave tequilas, they are also considered to be of lesser quality. To save money, choose a 100 percent agave blanco (not aged) instead of a mixto.

Ambassador

2 ounces tequila

1 teaspoon simple syrup

Orange juice to fill

Orange slice, for garnish (optional)

Pour the liquid ingredients into a highball glass over ice. Garnish with orange slice, if desired.

Astronaut Sunrise

1½ ounces tequila

½ ounce grenadine

Reconstituted Tang to fill

Fill a highball glass with ice, then pour in all the ingredients. Stir.

Black Turncoat

2 ounces tequila

Juice of ½ lime

Splash water

Cola to fill

1 lime twist, for garnish

Pour the tequila and lime juice into an old-fashioned glass over ice. Add a splash of water and stir. Top with soda. Garnish with lime twist.

Bloody Maria

2 ounces tequila

Bloody Mary mix to fill

1 celery stalk and lime wedge, for garnish (optional)

Pour the tequila into a highball glass of ice. Fill with Bloody Mary mix. Stir. Garnish with celery and lime wedge, if desired.

Jose Antonio de Cuervo

In 1758, Jose Antonio de Cuervo founded a distillery in the village of Tequila. Thirty-seven years later, his son Jose Guadalupe was granted the first license by the king of Spain to produce what was then called "wine of the earth."

Brave Bull

2 ounces tequila

1 ounce coffee liqueur

Pour the ingredients into an old-fashioned glass almost filled with ice. Stir well.

Cabo Wabo

1½ ounces tequila

¾ ounce Grand Marnier

1½ ounces sweet-and-sour mix

3 ounces cranberry juice

Splash Rose's lime juice

Combine the first four ingredients in a shaker with ice. Shake well. Strain into a cocktail glass. Finish with a splash of lime juice.

Cactus Bite

2 ounces tequila

¼ ounce triple sec

¼ ounce Drambuie

2 ounces lemon juice

½ teaspoon sugar

Dash bitters

Combine the ingredients in a shaker with ice. Shake well. Strain into a cocktail glass.

Dos Amigos Chicorita

Salt, for rimming (optional)

2 ounces tequila

1 ounce Grand Marnier

1½ ounces sweet-and-sour mix

1½ ounces orange juice

1 lime slice, for garnish

If desired, rim a cocktail glass with salt. Combine the liquid ingredients in a shaker with ice. Shake vigorously. Strain over ice into glass. Garnish with lime slice.

Dynamite

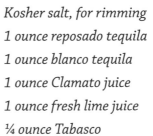

Kosher salt, for rimming

1 ounce reposado tequila

1 ounce blanco tequila

1 ounce Clamato juice

1 ounce fresh lime juice

¼ ounce Tabasco

Rim an old-fashioned glass with kosher salt. Fill the glass with ice and pour all ingredients in.

Exorcist

1½ ounces tequila

¾ ounce blue curaçao

¾ ounce lime juice

Combine the ingredients in a shaker with ice. Shake well. Strain into a cocktail glass.

Freddy Fudpucker

1 ounce tequila

Orange juice to fill

½ ounce Galliano to float

Pour the tequila into a highball glass filled with ice and fill with orange juice. Stir. Float the Galliano on top.

God Bless Texastini

1 ounce tequila

1 ounce Tequila Rose

1 ounce orange juice

1 ounce pineapple juice

Combine the ingredients in a shaker with ice. Shake well. Strain into a cocktail glass.

Word Meanings

Agave comes from a Greek word that means "noble." Tequila means "the rock that cuts." Most believe the name originated from the sharp rocks created by lava that surround the town of Tequila.

Guadalajara

2 ounces tequila

1 ounce dry vermouth

½ ounce Bénédictine

1 lemon twist, for garnish

Combine the ingredients in a shaker with ice. Stir well. Strain into a cocktail glass. Garnish with lemon twist.

La Bomba

1½ ounces tequila

½ ounce Cointreau

1 ounce pineapple juice

1 ounce orange juice

¼ ounce grenadine

Combine the ingredients in a shaker with ice. Shake well. Strain into a cocktail glass.

Margarita Name

There are many stories of how the Margarita got its name. One is that it was named after a Mexican bartender's girlfriend, Margarita. What we know for sure is that the Margarita is by far the most popular drink in the entire world.

Margarita

Kosher salt, for rimming

1½ ounces tequila

½ ounce Cointreau

1 ounce lime juice

½ ounce simple syrup

1 lime wedge or wheel, for garnish

Rim a large cocktail or margarita glass with salt. Add ice to the glass. Combine the liquid ingredients in a shaker with ice. Shake well. Strain into the glass. Garnish with lime wedge or wheel.

Margarita Blue

Salt, for rimming

1½ ounces tequila

½ ounce blue curaçao

1 teaspoon triple sec

1 ounce lime juice

1 lime wedge, for garnish

Rim a large cocktail or margarita glass with salt. Combine the liquid ingredients in a shaker half filled with ice. Shake well. Strain into the glass. Garnish with a lime wedge.

Massacre

2 ounces tequila

½ ounce Campari

4 ounces ginger ale

Pour all ingredients into a highball glass over ice. Stir well.

Mexican Madras

1 ounce tequila

1 ounce orange juice

3 ounces cranberry juice

¼ ounce lime juice

Combine the ingredients in a shaker half filled with ice. Shake well. Strain into a highball glass of ice.

Mexican Screw

1½ ounces tequila

Orange juice to fill

Pour both ingredients into a highball glass over ice. Stir.

Mexicana

2 ounces tequila

1 ounce pineapple juice

½ ounce lemon juice

1 teaspoon grenadine

Combine the ingredients in a shaker half filled with ice. Shake well. Strain into a cocktail glass.

Passion Cocktail

2 ounces tequila

3 ounces cranberry juice

1 ounce lime juice

2 ounces Grand Marnier

1 lime slice, for garnish

Combine the tequila and both juices in a shaker with ice. Shake well. Strain into a highball glass. Add the Grand Marnier. Garnish with slice of lime.

Petroleo

1 serrano chili, halved lengthwise and seeded (wash hands and kitchen tools immediately after seeding to avoid irritation)

2 ounces tequila

1 ounce lime juice

Dash salt and pepper

Splash Worcestershire sauce

Splash Maggi seasoning or soy sauce

Drop one of the chili halves into an old-fashioned glass. Fill the glass with ice. Put the rest of the ingredients into a shaker of ice (including the remaining chili half) and shake. Strain over the old-fashioned glass of ice.

Pink Tequila Sour

Kosher salt, for rimming

2 ounces gold tequila

1 ounce triple sec

1 ounce lime juice

¼ ounce orange juice

½ ounce simple syrup

¼ ounce grenadine

Rim a large cocktail or margarita glass with kosher salt and fill with ice. Combine the remaining ingredients in a shaker with ice. Shake well. Strain into the glass.

South of the Peachy Border Rita

Kosher salt, for rimming

1½ ounces tequila

1 ounce peach schnapps

⅛ ounce grenadine

3 ounces sweet-and-sour mix

1 lime wheel, for garnish

Rim a large cocktail or margarita glass with salt. Add ice. Combine the liquid ingredients in a shaker with ice. Shake well. Strain into the glass and garnish with lime wheel.

Swim-Up Bar Margarita

Kosher salt, for rimming

1½ ounces tequila

1 ounce blue curaçao

Juice from ½ lime

3 ounces sweet-and-sour mix

1 lime wheel, for garnish

Rim a large cocktail or margarita glass with salt and fill partway with ice. Combine the liquid ingredients in a shaker with ice. Shake well. Strain into the glass and garnish with lime wheel.

Tequila Canyon

1½ ounces tequila

¼ ounce triple sec

3 ounces cranberry juice

½ ounce pineapple juice

½ ounce orange juice

Pour the tequila, triple sec, and cranberry juice into a highball glass with ice. Add the pineapple and orange juice. Stir.

Tequila Manhattan

2 ounces tequila

¾ ounce sweet vermouth

1 cherry, for garnish (optional)

Combine the liquid ingredients in a shaker with ice. Shake well. Strain into a cocktail glass. Garnish with a cherry. Can also be served over ice in an old-fashioned glass.

Tequila Sunrise

1½ ounces tequila

½ ounce grenadine

Orange juice to fill

Pour the tequila and grenadine into a highball glass of ice. Fill with orange juice.

Tequila Sunrise Margarita

Kosher salt, for rimming

1½ ounces tequila

½ ounce grenadine

½ ounce triple sec

1 ounce sweet-and-sour mix

1 ounce orange juice

1 lime wheel, for garnish

Rim a large cocktail or margarita glass with salt. Add ice. Combine the liquid ingredients in a shaker with ice. Shake well. Strain into the glass and garnish with lime wheel.

The Tequila Sunrise Origins

The Tequila Sunrise was created in Mexico in the 1950s to welcome tourists to Acapulco and Cancun. The drink gained popularity again in the 1970s.

White Sangriarita

Kosher salt, for rimming

1½ ounces tequila

1 ounce white wine

4 ounces sweet-and-sour mix

Lime, orange, and lemon wheels, for garnish (optional)

Rim a cocktail or margarita glass with salt. Fill the glass with ice. Combine the tequila, white wine, and sweet-and-sour mix in a shaker with a cup of ice. Shake well. Strain into a large cocktail or margarita glass and float the citrus wheels on top, if desired.

11. Whiskey Cocktails

*F*our prominent countries—Scotland, Ireland, Canada, and the United States—produce whiskey, an alcohol distilled from fermented barley and other grains. Each country makes different types of whiskey. (Ireland and Scotland still argue over who made it first.) Ireland and the United States spell whiskey with an "e," while Canada and Scotland do not.

Whiskeys from different regions have strikingly different tastes. Local whiskeys go through an arduous process of distillation, fermentation, blending, and aging. Each whiskey region has its own techniques and traditions, which accounts for the vast difference in taste between Johnnie Walker and Jack Daniel's, for example.

Scotland produces blended Scotch whisky and single malt whisky. For a bottle to bear the "Scotch" label it must be made in Scotland. The single malt is made from a single distillation of malted barley, while the blended contains a combination of single malts and grain whiskys.

Ireland produces Irish whiskey, and there are only ten distilleries in operation or under construction. Irish whiskey comes in three types— pure pot still whiskey, single malt whiskey, and blended whiskey.

Canada produces blended whisky and rye whisky. Blended versions may combine many whiskys together to create a smooth-tasting final product.

America produces bourbon whiskey, corn whiskey, rye whiskey, blended whiskey, and Tennessee whiskey. High-end bourbon breaks down into two other categories called small batch bourbon and single barrel bourbon.

SCOTCH DISTINCTIONS

The different and distinctive tastes of Scotches are caused by the air quality, peat bogs, and water where the liquor is made, a fact that should make ardent environmentalists out of all Scotch drinkers. There are eight regions of single malt producers in Scotland, and the product of each is unique. Admirers of single malts are usually devotees of a particular brand. Enthusiasts of a blended label maintain that the art is in the blending. But few would deny the supremacy of Scotch in the domain of whisky.

Affinity

2 ounces blended Scotch whisky

1 ounce sweet vermouth

1 ounce dry vermouth

3 dashes bitters

Combine the ingredients in a shaker with ice. Shake well. Strain into a cocktail glass.

Aggravation

2 ounces blended Scotch whisky

1 ounce coffee liqueur

Pour the ingredients into an old-fashioned glass of ice and stir.

Balmoral

2 ounces blended Scotch whisky

½ ounce sweet vermouth

½ ounce dry vermouth

2 dashes bitters

Combine the ingredients in a mixing glass half filled with ice. Stir and strain into a cocktail glass.

Bobby Burns

1½ ounces blended Scotch whisky

1½ ounces sweet vermouth

1 teaspoon Bénédictine

Pour the ingredients into a mixing glass nearly filled with ice. Stir and strain into a cocktail glass.

Borden Chase

2 ounces Scotch

½ ounce dry vermouth

¼ ounce absinthe

2 dashes orange bitters

Combine the ingredients in a shaker with ice. Shake well. Strain into a chilled cocktail glass.

Godfather

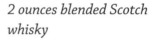

2 ounces blended Scotch whisky

¾ ounce amaretto

Pour the Scotch and amaretto into an old-fashioned glass over ice.

Rusty Nail

1½ ounces Scotch

½ ounce Drambuie

Pour the ingredients into an old-fashioned glass of ice.

Scotch Sour

1½ ounces blended Scotch whisky

1 ounce lemon juice

Combine the ingredients in a shaker half filled with ice. Shake well. Strain into an old-fashioned glass of ice.

Smoke and Mirrors

2 ounces Scotch

1 ounce absinthe

½ ounce simple syrup

½ ounce fresh lime juice

Combine the ingredients in a shaker with ice. Shake well. Strain into an old-fashioned glass with ice.

Irish whiskey comes in several forms. There is a single malt whiskey made from 100 percent malted barley distilled in a pot still, and a grain whiskey made from grains distilled in a column still. Grain whiskey is much lighter and more neutral in flavor than single malt whiskey and is almost never bottled as a single grain. It is instead used to blend with single malts to produce a lighter blended whiskey. Unique to Irish whiskey is pure pot still whiskey (100 percent barley, both malted and unmalted, distilled in a pot still). The green, unmalted barley gives pure pot still whiskey a spicy, uniquely Irish quality. Like single malt, pure pot still is sold alone or blended with grain whiskey. Usually no real distinction is made between blended whiskeys made from single malt or pure pot still.

Black Thorn

1 ounce Irish whiskey

1 ounce dry vermouth

3 dashes Pernod

3 dashes bitters

Combine the ingredients in a shaker with ice. Stir well. Strain into an old-fashioned glass of ice.

Brainstorm

2 ounces Irish whiskey

¼ ounce sweet vermouth

¼ ounce Bénédictine

Dash Angostura bitters

Combine the ingredients in a shaker with ice. Shake well. Strain into a chilled cocktail glass.

Irish Coffee

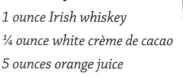

6 ounces coffee

1½ ounces Irish whiskey

1 teaspoon brown sugar

Whipped cream, for garnish (optional)

Preheat an Irish coffee mug with hot water. Pour out the water and add coffee until the mug is three-quarters full, about 6 ounces. Add the whiskey and brown sugar and stir. Fill to the top with whipped cream, if desired.

> **Irish Coffee Cake**
>
> Add some kick to a brunch staple by soaking a coffee cake in a syrup made of Irish whiskey, coffee, and sugar.

Irish Magic

1 ounce Irish whiskey

¼ ounce white crème de cacao

5 ounces orange juice

Pour all ingredients over ice in a highball glass and stir.

Irish Rickey

1½ ounces Irish whiskey

Juice from ½ lime

Club soda to fill

Pour the Irish whiskey and lime juice into a highball glass of ice. Top with club soda.

Irish Shillelagh

1½ ounces Irish whiskey

Juice from ½ lemon

1 teaspoon powdered sugar

1 tablespoon sloe gin

1 tablespoon light rum

Combine the ingredients in a shaker with ice. Shake well. Strain into an old-fashioned glass of ice.

The First Whiskey?

Irish whiskey is believed to be one of the earliest distilled beverages in Europe, dating to the mid-twelfth century. The Old Bushmills Distillery lays claim to being the oldest licensed distillery in the world. James I awarded the distillery its license in 1608.

Paddy Cocktail

2 ounces Irish whiskey

2 or 3 dashes Angostura bitters

¾ ounce sweet vermouth

Pour all ingredients into an old-fashioned glass of ice and stir.

It's no surprise that the Mint Julep and bourbon have the same home territory—Bourbon County, Kentucky. Bourbon whiskey, born in the late 1700s, is America's original native brew. Bourbon's distinctive flavor emerges from its mash, which is at least 51 percent corn, and the charred oak barrels in which the liquor ages. A mash, the source of all whiskeys and beers, is milled cereal cooked in water. The quality of that water is all-important. Eighty percent of the world's bourbon is produced in America because of the clear limestone spring water of the Kentucky hills. People think that Jack Daniel's Tennessee whiskey gets its flavor from being a sour mash. Wrong! Many whiskeys are made from a sour mash. JD gets its flavor from dripping through ten feet of sugar maple charcoal before it's put into charred barrels.

Canadian whisky production grew tremendously because of the American Prohibition. Windsor, Ontario, supplied its upriver neighbors in Detroit, Michigan, with alcohol, and the porous United States–Canadian border allowed for a steady trade between the two countries. Today, the most popular Canadian whiskys are Crown Royal, Canadian Club, Seagram's V.O., and Black Velvet.

If you and your guests are big fans of whiskey, your bar cart can soon be overrun by bottles representing the various options, defeating the whole purpose of a bar cart (which is to keep it simple!). So, when stocking your bar cart, remember that a guest who likes bourbon probably won't say no to whiskey, and vice versa. Choose a good bottle of whatever type of whiskey (or whisky or scotch or bourbon) that you like best. If you feel the need, supplement it with a special bottle of single-malt scotch. And you're good to go!

Ace of Royal Spades

1 ounce Crown Royal Canadian whisky

1 ounce amaretto

Cola to fill

Pour the Crown Royal and amaretto into a highball glass of ice. Fill with cola.

> **Bourbon: American Made**
>
> By law, bourbon can only be made in America, and a label can only say "Kentucky bourbon" if it's made in Kentucky.

Admiral

1 ounce rye whiskey

2 ounces dry vermouth

½ ounce lemon juice

1 lemon twist, for garnish

Combine the ingredients in a shaker with ice. Shake well. Strain into an old-fashioned glass. Garnish with lemon twist.

Agent Orange

1 ounce Tennessee whiskey

1 ounce Southern Comfort

Orange juice to fill

Pour the whiskey and Southern Comfort into a highball glass of ice. Fill with orange juice.

Algonquin

1½ ounces rye whiskey

1 ounce dry vermouth

1 ounce pineapple juice

Combine the ingredients in a shaker half filled with ice. Shake well. Strain into an old-fashioned glass of ice.

All American

1 ounce bourbon

1 ounce Southern Comfort

2 ounces cola

Pour all ingredients in an old-fashioned glass and stir.

Kentucky Whisky

America spells whiskey with the "e." However, Kentucky spells it without the "e." This is because Kentucky whisky is made Scottish style using cold winter wheat instead of summer wheat. By doing this, Kentucky honors the Scottish ways and uses the Scottish spelling as well.

Bourbon and Branch

2 ounces bourbon

Still mineral water to fill

Pour the bourbon into an old-fashioned glass of ice. Fill with water.

Bourbon Daisy

1½ ounces bourbon

½ ounce lemon juice

1 teaspoon grenadine

Club soda to fill

¼ ounce Southern Comfort, to float

1 orange slice and 1 pineapple stick, for garnish (optional)

Shake the bourbon, lemon juice, and grenadine with ice. Strain into a highball glass of ice. Fill with club soda and float the Southern Comfort. Garnish with the orange slice and pineapple stick, if desired.

Elijah Craig

Elijah Craig, a Baptist preacher, was the first to discover that aging whiskey in charred barrels changed the flavor and color of the drink. The only barrels he could afford in the beginning were used herring barrels, so he'd torch the insides to burn the fish smell out of them. Today, all whiskey factories char their oak barrels.

California Lemonade

2 ounces blended whiskey

1 tablespoon sugar

1 ounce lemon juice

1 ounce lime juice

Club soda to fill

1 lemon wedge, for garnish

Combine the first four ingredients in a shaker half filled with ice. Shake well. Strain into a highball glass of ice. Fill with club soda and garnish with lemon wedge.

Canadian Cocktail

1½ ounces Canadian whisky

½ ounce Cointreau

1 teaspoon sugar

Dash bitters

Combine the ingredients in a shaker half filled with ice. Shake well. Strain into a cocktail glass.

Commodore

2 ounces rye whiskey

1 ounce fresh lemon juice

1 ounce simple syrup

2 dashes orange bitters

Combine the ingredients in a shaker with ice. Shake well. Strain into a cocktail glass.

Double Standard Sour

1 ounce blended whiskey

1 ounce gin

½ ounce lemon or lime juice

1 teaspoon fine sugar

½ teaspoon grenadine

1 lemon twist and 1 cherry for garnish (optional)

Combine the ingredients, except garnish, in a shaker with ice. Shake well. Strain into a highball glass. Garnish with lemon and cherry, if desired.

Esquire

2 ounces bourbon

½ ounce Grand Marnier

½ ounce fresh orange juice

¼ ounce fresh lemon juice

2 dashes Angostura bitters

1 lemon twist, for garnish

Combine the liquid ingredients in a shaker with ice. Shake well. Strain into a cocktail glass. Garnish with lemon twist.

John Collins

2 ounces rye whiskey

½ ounce lemon juice

½ ounce simple syrup

Club soda to fill

1 orange slice and 1 cherry, for garnish (optional)

Shake the first three ingredients. Strain into a highball glass of ice. Fill with club soda. Garnish with orange and cherry, if desired.

J.R.'s Godfather

2 ounces bourbon

½ ounce amaretto

Pour the bourbon and amaretto into an old-fashioned glass of ice. Stir well.

Kentucky

2 ounces bourbon

1 ounce pineapple juice

Combine the ingredients in a shaker with ice. Shake well. Strain into a cocktail glass.

Kentucky Colonel

1½ ounces bourbon

½ ounce Bénédictine

1 lemon twist, for garnish

Combine the bourbon and Bénédictine in a mixing glass half filled with ice. Stir, then strain into a cocktail glass. Serve with a lemon twist.

Leatherneck

2 ounces blended whiskey

¾ ounce blue curaçao

½ ounce fresh lime juice

1 lime wheel, for garnish

Combine the liquid ingredients in a shaker with ice. Shake well. Strain into a cocktail glass. Garnish with lime wheel.

Lynchburg Lemonade

1½ ounces Jack Daniel's whiskey

½ ounce triple sec

2 ounces sweet-and-sour mix

Sprite or 7Up to fill

1 lemon wedge, for garnish

Pour the first three ingredients into a highball glass of ice. Fill with Sprite or 7Up. Garnish with lemon wedge.

Manhattan

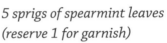

2 ounces rye whiskey

½ ounce sweet vermouth

2 dashes Angostura bitters

1 cherry, for garnish (optional)

Combine the liquid ingredients in a shaker with ice. Shake well. Strain into a cocktail glass. Garnish with cherry. Manhattans can also be served on the rocks.

The Manhattan Project

It is believed that a bartender at a party hosted by Winston Churchill's mother invented the Manhattan. The party was at the Manhattan Club in New York City.

The Mint Julep

The Mint Julep is the official drink of the Kentucky Derby. The cocktail, served in a traditional silver cup and garnished with bourbon-infused mint, should be stirred until frost forms on the outside of the cup.

Mint Julep

5 sprigs of spearmint leaves (reserve 1 for garnish)

1 tablespoon sugar

2 ounces bourbon

Muddle 4 spearmint sprigs and the sugar in a highball glass. Fill with ice. Add the bourbon and stir until glass gets very cold. Add more ice if needed. Garnish with remaining sprig.

Old-Fashioned

1 tablespoon sugar

1 orange slice

1 cherry

2 dashes Angostura bitters

2 ounces rye, bourbon, or whiskey

Muddle the sugar, orange slice, cherry, and bitters in an old-fashioned glass. Fill with ice. Add the rye, bourbon, or whiskey.

Old Pal

1 ounce Canadian whisky

1 ounce dry vermouth

1 ounce Campari

Pour the ingredients into an old-fashioned glass of ice and stir.

Seven and Seven

2 ounces Seagram's 7

7Up or Sprite to fill

Pour the liquor into a highball glass of ice. Fill with soda.

Whiskey Sour

2 ounces bourbon or whiskey

1 ounce lemon juice

1 ounce simple syrup

Combine the ingredients in a shaker with ice. Shake well. Strain into an old-fashioned glass of ice.

12. Shots and Shooters

*S*hots and shooters are meant to be drunk very quickly in one gulp. They can measure from 1 ounce up to almost 4 ounces and are served in shot glasses, liqueur glasses, shooter glasses, or old-fashioned glasses. The difference between a shot and a shooter is based on the alcohol content. For example, a shot of tequila and an Alabama Slammer shot are both pure alcohol, so they are shots. A Blue Marlin Shooter and a Red Snapper have nonalcoholic mixers added to them, so they are shooters.

A classic image of downing shots comes from old Western movies when a cowboy would stroll into the local saloon. Things were simple—just beer and shots. Ancient diggings reveal that shots have been around a lot longer than that. In 1982, a Tang dynasty (C.E. 618–907) vessel used for drinking games was unearthed in Dantu county in Jiangsu province. It has a tortoise-shaped pedestal and a barrel to hold liquor. It's inscribed with a quotation from the *Analects of Confucius*—an instruction to drink, persuade others to drink, punish, or let go. It's believed to be a drinking game relic.

Shots and shooters can be prepared one of three ways: neat, layered, and chilled straight up. Types and names for shots and shooters can be shot, shooter, drop, bomb, and slammer. Drops and bombs refer to a shot of something being dropped into a glass of something else and then chugged. A slammer is slammed down on the table, and you drink it while it fizzes. Shots and shooters can also be layered or flamed.

You don't need a lot of special equipment to serve shots and shooters—there are plenty of options that don't require you to make and refrigerate Jell-O. Know that you can make a shooter from practically any popular drink by reducing the amount of mixer. So, the ingredients you already have on your bar cart may be all you need to enjoy shots and shooters with your friends. If not, pick one or two favorite shots and then stock the ingredients you'll need for those drinks.

Alabama Slammer Shot

⅓ ounce Southern Comfort

⅓ ounce amaretto

⅓ ounce sloe gin

Combine the ingredients in a shaker. Shake well. Strain into a shot glass.

Anita Rita Now

1½ ounces tequila

¾ ounce triple sec

½ ounce lime juice

3 ounces limeade

Pour the tequila in a shot glass. Pour the triple sec and the lime juice in another shot glass. Pour the limeade in an old-fashioned glass. Then drink each one right after the other. That is the fastest Rita when you need a Rita now!

B-52

½ ounce coffee liqueur

½ ounce Irish cream

½ ounce Grand Marnier

Into a shot glass, layer each ingredient in order with a spoon.

Baileys Comet

1½ ounces Baileys Irish Cream liqueur

⅛ ounce 151 rum

Pinch of cinnamon

Pour the Baileys into a shot glass. Float the rum on top. Light the rum. Sprinkle cinnamon over the flame to create tiny firework-like sparkles (the comet effect). Allow the flames to die, then drink. Be careful of the glass's hot rim.

Flaming Shots and Shooters

Flamed shots and shooters are set on fire, and much precaution should always be taken when playing with fire. Always make sure everything in the area around and above you is nonflammable. Flames should be blown out before the shot ever reaches your mouth. And always light the shot with a match as opposed to a lighter. With a lighter, you risk contaminating your shot with lighter fluid.

Bet the Limit

½ shot tequila

½ shot Cointreau

Combine the ingredients in a shaker with ice. Stir well. Strain into a shot glass.

Blue Marlin Shooter

1 ounce light rum

½ ounce blue curaçao

1 ounce lime juice

Pour the ingredients into a mixing glass half filled with ice. Stir. Strain into a large shot, shooter, or old-fashioned glass.

Brain Hemorrhage

1 ounce peach schnapps

¼ ounce Irish cream

¼ ounce grenadine

First, pour the peach schnapps into a shot glass. Slowly add the Irish cream, and it will clump and settle at the bottom. Next, slowly pour the grenadine to give it a bloody, disgusting brain-hemorrhage look.

Burning Busch

1 bottle Busch beer

1 ounce Southern Comfort

⅛ ounce 151 rum

Pour a bottle of Busch beer into a pint glass. In a shot glass, pour in the Southern Comfort and carefully layer the 151 rum on top. Light the shot and let it burn for a bit to burn most of the rum away. Drop into the beer and chug.

Cement Mixer

1½ ounces Irish cream

¼ ounce Rose's lime juice

This is a gag shooter. Pour the ingredients into a shot glass and drink. It curdles in your mouth.

Cigar Band

½ ounce amaretto

½ ounce Irish cream

½ ounce cognac

Into a shot glass, layer each ingredient in order with a spoon.

Dragon's Breath

½ ounce green crème de menthe

½ ounce gold tequila

⅛ ounce Grand Marnier

Into a shot glass, carefully layer each ingredient in order with a spoon. Light the Grand Marnier with a match; allow the flame to die out, then drink.

Falling Star

1 ounce bourbon

1 ounce sambuca

Combine the ingredients in a shaker with ice. Shake well. Strain into a shot glass.

Kamikaze

1½ ounces vodka

½ ounce triple sec

¼ ounce lime juice

Shake and strain into a large shot, shooter, or old-fashioned glass.

Lemon Drop Shooter

Sugar, for rimming

½ ounce triple sec

1½ ounces lemon vodka

1 ounce sweet-and-sour mix

Rim a shot glass or old-fashioned glass with sugar. Shake and strain remaining ingredients into glass. You can also try it with mandarin, mango, pear, pomegranate, or melon vodka.

Shooters of Yesterday

Today anything poured into a martini glass is called a Martini. Just know that the chugged shooters of yesterday are really just the flavored Martinis you sip today. A real Martini is gin and dry vermouth. Period.

Lunch Box

3½ ounces orange juice

1½ ounces beer

1½ ounces amaretto

1½ ounces Southern Comfort

Pour the orange juice and beer into a highball glass. Then take a shot glass and pour in the amaretto and Southern Comfort. Drop the shot glass into the highball glass, then chug.

Mind Eraser

1 ounce vodka

1 ounce coffee liqueur

Club soda to fill

Pour the first two ingredients into an old-fashioned glass of ice. Fill with club soda. Stick in a straw and drink all at once.

Orgasm Shot

⅓ ounce amaretto

⅓ ounce coffee liqueur

⅓ ounce Irish cream

Shake ingredients and strain into a large shot, shooter, or old-fashioned glass.

Prairie Fire Shooter

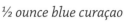

1½ ounces tequila

3 dashes Tabasco

Pour the tequila into a shot glass and add the Tabasco.

Psycho Tsunami

½ ounce blue curaçao

½ ounce lime juice

½ ounce tequila

2 dashes Tabasco sauce

Pour the ingredients into a shot glass. Allow Tabasco to settle before drinking.

Python

10–15 dashes Tabasco

½ shot whiskey

½ shot tequila

Put Tabasco into shot glass. Top with whiskey and tequila.

Rat Pack

½ ounce Jack Daniel's whiskey

½ ounce Johnnie Walker Scotch

½ ounce coffee liqueur

Combine the ingredients in a shaker with ice. Shake well. Strain into a shot glass.

Red Snapper

1 ounce Crown Royal

1 ounce amaretto

2 ounces cranberry juice

Shake ingredients and strain into a large shot, shooter, or old-fashioned glass.

Russian Quaalude

⅓ ounce vodka

⅓ ounce Irish cream

⅓ ounce Frangelico

Shake ingredients and strain into a shot glass.

Sammy Jäger

1 ounce sambuca

1 ounce Jägermeister

Shake ingredients and strain into a shot glass.

Screaming Orgasm

¼ ounce vodka

¼ ounce amaretto

¼ ounce coffee liqueur

¼ ounce Irish cream

Shake ingredients and strain into a large shot, shooter, or old-fashioned glass.

Slippery Nipple

¾ ounce sambuca

¾ ounce Irish cream

Into a shot glass, layer each ingredient in order with a spoon.

Snowshoe

¾ ounce Wild Turkey

¾ ounce peppermint schnapps

Shake ingredients and strain into a large shot, shooter, or old-fashioned glass.

Layered Shots

Liqueurs have different densities, so it's possible to carefully layer them to create a rainbow or striped effect. The official name for this technique is pousse-café.

SoCo and Lime

2 ounces Southern Comfort

½ ounce Rose's lime juice

Shake ingredients and strain into a large shot, shooter, or old-fashioned glass.

Statue of Liberty

⅓ ounce grenadine

⅓ ounce blue curaçao

⅓ ounce white crème de cacao

⅛ ounce 151 rum

Into a shot glass, carefully layer each ingredient in order with a spoon. Light, hold up like the Statue of Liberty, blow out the flame, and drink. It will taste like a chocolate-covered cherry.

Shooter Pyramid

Why not make a shooter pyramid out of six shooters? Three glasses will be on the bottom, two balanced on top of the space between those, and then one on top. You have to curve the pattern in order to strain the liquid into all the glasses.

Tequila Slammer

1½ ounces tequila

2 ounces Sprite or 7Up

Pour the ingredients into an old-fashioned glass, place a napkin over the glass, and slam glass on the table or bar top so that it fizzes. Drink.

Three Wise Men

½ ounce Johnnie Walker Scotch whisky

½ ounce Jim Beam bourbon whiskey

½ ounce Jack Daniel's Tennessee whiskey

Shake ingredients and strain into a shot glass.

Three Wise Men Go Hunting

½ ounce Johnnie Walker Scotch whisky

½ ounce Jim Beam bourbon whiskey

½ ounce Jack Daniel's Tennessee whiskey

½ ounce Wild Turkey bourbon whiskey

Shake ingredients and strain into a shot glass.

Three Wise Men Visit Mexico

½ ounce Johnnie Walker Scotch whisky

½ ounce Jim Beam bourbon whiskey

½ ounce Jack Daniel's Tennessee whiskey

½ ounce Jose Cuervo Gold tequila

Shake ingredients and strain into a shot glass.

Drops and Bombs

The original name for Drops and Bombs is a Boilermaker (shot of whiskey dropped into a beer). The words drops and bombs gained popularity about a decade ago.

Woo Woo

1 ounce vodka

1 ounce peach schnapps

1 ounce cranberry juice

Shake ingredients and strain into a large shot, shooter, or old-fashioned glass.

13. Multi-Spirited Specialty Drinks

A Long Island Iced Tea recipe calls for vodka, gin, rum, tequila, and triple sec. Which chapter should the recpie be in? You see the dilemma. The recipes in this chapter are multi-spirited. You'll find classic, tropical, hot, juicy, creamy, and sour recipes all living together here. But what you won't find is a lot of fuss. That's contrary to the bar cart ethos! You don't need blenders and microwaves and complicated equipment to mix a good drink.

Popular lore says that one of the first cocktails was a multi-spirited drink, mixed in New Orleans in the early 1800s. The Sazerac was made with rye whiskey, absinthe, bitters, and sugar. There have been many punches and sangrias since then, but it's believed that the multi-spirited seed was planted when TGI Fridays opened the first casual bar and grill in New York City in 1965. Fridays was first to create a cocktail menu to go alongside the food menu, a tradition it proudly carries on today.

By the late 1970s, hundreds of imitative bar and grills opened nationwide, and all had menus advertising multi-spirited drinks full of the flavors of the time: coffee liqueur, Irish cream, amaretto, blue curaçao, crème de cacao, flavored brandies, and grenadine. Between the 1980s and 2000s the menu choices exploded, thanks to a glut of new products flooding the market, including schnapps in all flavors, crème liqueurs in all flavors, and every category of spirit infused with every flavor imaginable.

Multi-spirited drink recipes assume that your bar cart is well stocked with different types of alcohol, from tequila to rum to whiskey. But because the bar cart is about selection, the recipes here are tailored for the discerning drinker. You may need one or two specialty ingredients to make a bar cart multi-spirited drink, but not seven. Use the recipes that work best with your bar cart sensibilities and enjoy!

AK-47

¼ ounce brandy

¼ ounce whiskey

¼ ounce gin

¼ ounce vodka

¼ ounce rum

¼ ounce bourbon

¼ ounce Cointreau

1 ounce lime juice

Club soda to fill

Pour the liquors and lime juice into a highball glass of ice. Fill with club soda.

Alpine Lemonade

1 ounce vodka

1 ounce gin

1 ounce rum

Lemonade and cranberry juice to fill

Pour the vodka, gin, and rum into a highball glass of ice. Fill with equal parts of lemonade and cranberry juice.

Alternatini

3 ounces vodka

¼ ounce white crème de cacao

¼ ounce sweet vermouth

¼ ounce dry vermouth

Combine the ingredients in a shaker with ice. Shake well. Strain into a cocktail glass.

Vermouth

Vermouth is a fortified wine flavored with herbs, spices, barks, and flowers. The flavors can be added through infusion, maceration, or distillation. There are many brands of vermouth produced in both Italy and France.

Angel's Fall

1 ounce amaretto

½ ounce gin

½ ounce vodka

½ ounce 151 rum

½ ounce dark rum

1 ounce grenadine

Cranberry, pineapple, and grapefruit juice to fill

Pour the liquors and grenadine into a highball glass of ice. Fill with equal parts of cranberry, pineapple, and grapefruit juice.

Assassin

⅓ ounce Jack Daniel's whiskey

⅓ ounce tequila

⅓ ounce peppermint schnapps

Pour the ingredients into a cocktail glass. Stir well.

What Is Schnapps?

Liqueurs are made by steeping herbs and fruits in an alcohol that had already been fermented and distilled. But schnapps is made from grains, fruit, or herbs fermented and distilled together. This is the reason schnapps can have a high alcohol content.

Asylum

1 ounce absinthe

1 ounce gin

¼ ounce grenadine

Pour all ingredients into an old-fashioned glass of ice. Stir.

Hallucinogenic Alcohol

Absinthe (AB-sinth) has a dark, dangerous history. It was one of the ingredients in what is believed to be the world's first cocktail, the Sazerac. This pastis had a high alcohol content and was made with wormwood, which caused slight hallucinations, earning it the nickname the Green Fairy (*La Fée Verte*). By 1906, absinthe was banned in Brazil and Belgium. It was eventually outlawed worldwide except in England, Sweden, and Norway. In July 2007, New Orleans absinthe historian, chemist, and environmental microbiologist T.A. Breaux lobbied the American Congress into allowing the first legal absinthe (after being banned for 95 years) into America. The name of this absinthe is Lucid.

Barbary Coast

½ ounce Scotch

½ ounce gin

½ ounce rum

½ ounce white crème de cacao

½ ounce cream

Combine the ingredients in a shaker with ice. Shake well. Strain into a cocktail glass.

Barracuda Bite

1½ ounces 151 rum

1½ ounces vodka

½ ounce grenadine

½ ounce lime juice

Combine the ingredients in a shaker with ice. Stir gently. Strain into a highball glass over ice.

Chatham Hotel Special

1½ ounces brandy

½ ounce ruby port

¼ ounce dark crème de cacao

½ ounce cream

Combine the ingredients in a shaker with ice. Shake well. Strain into a cocktail glass.

Delmonico

1 ounce gin

1 ounce brandy

½ ounce dry vermouth

½ ounce sweet vermouth

1 dash orange bitters

1 lemon twist, for garnish

Combine the ingredients in a shaker with ice. Stir well. Strain into a cocktail glass. Garnish with lemon twist.

Down Under

½ ounce blue curaçao

¼ ounce rum

¼ ounce tequila

¼ ounce triple sec

¼ ounce vodka

1½ ounces club soda

Pour the first five ingredients into a highball glass over ice. Add the soda to fill. Stir.

Cocktails in the Sky

The first in-flight cocktails were served to paying passengers on the Zeppelin (airship) flying over Germany. The year was 1910.

El Chico

1½ *ounces light rum*

½ *ounce sweet vermouth*

¼ *teaspoon grenadine*

¼ *teaspoon curaçao*

1 *cherry and 1 lemon twist, for garnish (optional)*

Combine the liquid ingredients in a shaker nearly filled with ice. Shake well. Strain into a cocktail glass. Serve with cherry and lemon twist, if desired.

Electric Iced Tea

½ *ounce vodka*

½ *ounce gin*

½ *ounce rum*

½ *ounce tequila*

½ *ounce blue curaçao*

1 *ounce sour mix*

Splash Sprite or 7Up

Pour all ingredients into a highball glass of ice. Stir.

El Presidente

1½ *ounces light rum*

¾ *ounce curaçao*

¾ *ounce dry vermouth*

¼ *ounce grenadine*

Combine the ingredients in a shaker with ice. Shake well. Strain into a cocktail glass.

Fiery Sunset Tea

½ ounce vodka

½ ounce gin

½ ounce rum

½ ounce tequila

½ ounce triple sec

Sweet-and-sour mix to fill

1 ounce cranberry juice

½ ounce 151 rum

Pour the vodka, gin, rum, tequila, and triple sec into an ice-filled highball glass. Add the sweet-and-sour mix to nearly fill. Stir. Top first with cranberry juice, then with 151 rum. Ignite the rum. Make sure the fire has died out and the rim of the glass has cooled before taking a drink.

Floridita

1½ ounces rum

½ ounce sweet vermouth

⅛ ounce white crème de cacao

½ ounce lime juice

⅛ ounce grenadine

Combine the ingredients in a shaker with ice. Shake well. Strain into a cocktail glass.

Graveyard

¼ ounce triple sec

¼ ounce rum

¼ ounce vodka

¼ ounce gin

¼ ounce tequila

¼ ounce bourbon whiskey

¼ ounce scotch

Several ounces pilsner-style beer

Several ounces stout

Pour the liquors into a pint glass. Fill with half beer and half stout.

Hand Grenade

1 ounce 151 rum

1 ounce vodka

1 ounce melon liqueur, such as Midori

1 ounce amaretto

Pineapple juice to fill

Pour the first four ingredients into a highball glass of ice. Fill with pineapple juice.

Long Beach Tea

½ ounce vodka

½ ounce gin

½ ounce light rum

½ ounce tequila

½ ounce triple sec

1 ounce sour mix

1 ounce cranberry juice

Pour all ingredients into a highball glass of ice. Stir.

Long Island Iced Tea

½ ounce vodka

½ ounce light rum

½ ounce tequila

½ ounce triple sec

½ ounce gin

1 ounce sour mix

Splash of cola

Pour all ingredients into a highball glass of ice. Stir.

The Origins of the Long Island Iced Tea (LIIT)

Some cocktail historians claim the LIIT was created during Prohibition as a way to disguise an alcoholic beverage as a nonalcoholic drink (iced tea). However, others say it was invented in the mid-1970s by a bartender from Long Island, New York. TGI Fridays says it was responsible for the classic drink. LIIT was a big hit during the disco years (and still is).

Man Hunting

1½ ounces Wild Turkey 101

1 ounce curaçao

½ ounce sweet vermouth

½ ounce lemon juice

Combine the ingredients in a shaker with ice. Shake well. Strain into a cocktail glass.

Miami Iced Tea

½ ounce vodka

½ ounce gin

½ ounce light rum

½ ounce peach schnapps

½ ounce triple sec

1 ounce sour mix

1 ounce cranberry juice

Splash Sprite or 7Up

Pour all ingredients into a highball glass of ice. Stir.

Miami Vice

The Miami Iced Tea is not the same as a Miami Vice. A Miami Vice is half Strawberry Daiquiri and half Piña Colada.

Port Authority

2 ounces port wine

1 ounce Grand Marnier

½ ounce amaretto

Pour all ingredients into an old-fashioned glass of ice and stir.

Red Death

¾ ounce vodka

¾ ounce Southern Comfort

¼ ounce sloe gin

¼ ounce triple sec

¼ ounce Rose's lime juice

¼ ounce grenadine

Orange juice to fill

Pour the liquors, lime juice, and grenadine into a highball glass of ice. Fill with orange juice.

Snakebite

1½ ounces Jack Daniel's whiskey

1½ ounces tequila

1½ ounces Southern Comfort

Shake ingredients with ice and strain into an old-fashioned glass.

Tango

½ ounce rum

½ ounce sweet vermouth

½ ounce dry vermouth

½ ounce Bénédictine

1 ounce orange juice

Combine the ingredients in a shaker with ice. Shake well. Strain into a cocktail glass.

Texas Tea

½ ounce tequila

½ ounce vodka

½ ounce rum

½ ounce triple sec

1 ounce sour mix

Splash of cola

Pour all ingredients into a highball glass of ice. Stir.

Tropical Iced Tea

½ ounce vodka

½ ounce rum

½ ounce gin

½ ounce triple sec

1 ounce sweet-and-sour mix

1 ounce pineapple juice

1 ounce cranberry juice

½ ounce grenadine

Seasonal fruits, for garnish (optional)

Pour all ingredients into highball glass over ice. Garnish with seasonal fruits, if desired.

Tropical Itch

1 ounce dark rum

1 ounce American whiskey

1 ounce triple sec

4 ounces orange juice

1 pineapple slice and 1 cherry, for garnish (optional)

Shake the liquid ingredients with ice and strain into a highball glass of fresh ice. Garnish with the pineapple and cherry, if desired.

Twelve Mile Limit

1 ounce light rum

½ ounce rye whiskey

½ ounce brandy

½ ounce grenadine

½ fresh lemon juice

1 lemon twist, for garnish

Combine the liquid ingredients in a shaker with ice. Shake well. Strain into a cocktail glass. Garnish with lemon twist.

Uno Cinco de Mayo Rita

Salt for rimming (optional)

½ ounce tequila

½ ounce triple sec

½ ounce vodka

½ ounce gin

½ ounce rum

Sweet-and-sour mix to fill

1 lime slice, for garnish

Rim cocktail glass with salt, if desired. Pour the tequila, triple sec, vodka, gin, and rum into glass over ice. Stir. Add sweet-and-sour mix to fill. Garnish with lime slice.

14. Seasonal Cocktails

*H*umans will find just about any reason, season, or holiday to celebrate. Be prepared by changing up how you stock your bar cart, depending on the season. In the fall, you'll want cider on hand; in the winter, cocoa. In the spring, break out the Irish cream, and in the summer, make sure you have plenty of coconut rum aboard.

Stocking your bar cart for seasons, holidays, and occasions also gives you and your guests a chance to try out new drink recipes and spirits while still keeping your ingredients smartly curated. Your bar cart can't be all things to all people all the time, but with seasonal strategizing, you can avoid getting stuck in a rut.

> **Party Tip**
> Know that any single drink made from a recipe in this chapter can be mass-produced.

JANUARY–APRIL

These recipes cover seasons and holidays in January, February, March, and April.

Chinese New Year Champagne

½ ounce lychee liqueur

½ ounce tangerine juice

Champagne to fill

Pour the lychee liqueur and tangerine juice into a champagne flute, then add the champagne.

Green Beer (St. Patrick's Day)

1 pint pilsner (yellow beer)

1 drop green food coloring

Pour up a pint of beer, then add 1 drop green food coloring.

Kama Sutra (Valentine's Day)

½ ounce passion fruit liqueur

½ ounce Alizé Red Passion

½ ounce DeKuyper Cheri-Beri Pucker

Ginger ale to fill

Maraschino cherries, for garnish

Pour the first three ingredients into a highball glass, then add ice. Fill to the top with ginger ale and garnish with maraschino cherries.

Kiss from a Rose (Valentine's Day)

1 ounce rosé wine

1 ounce Tequila Rose

2 ounces cream

Combine the ingredients in a shaker with ice. Shake well. Strain into a cocktail glass.

Nutty Irishmantini (St. Patrick's Day)

1 ounce Irish cream

1 ounce Frangelico

½ ounce Irish whiskey

1 ounce cream

Combine the ingredients in a shaker with ice. Shake well. Strain into a cocktail glass.

Sparkling New Year Cheer

1 sugar cube

6 dashes Angostura bitters

Chilled champagne to fill

1 lemon twist

Dash the sugar cube with Angostura bitters and drop into the bottom of a champagne flute. Fill the flute with champagne. Twist a lemon twist to release the oils, then rub the rim of the glass with the twist and drop it into the drink.

Super Bowl Drop Kick

1 glass beer of your choice

1 ounce American whiskey

Fill a pint glass with a beer, then pour the American whiskey into a shot glass. Here's where the drop kick comes in: Drop the shot into the beer and kick the whole thing (beer and all) down your throat in one fell swoop.

White Chocolate Eastertini

1 ounce vanilla vodka

1 ounce white chocolate liqueur

2 ounces eggnog

1 ounce cream

Jellybeans, for garnish

Combine the liquids in a shaker with ice. Shake well. Strain into a large cocktail glass. Hide your little Easter eggs by dropping some jellybeans in the glass to sink to the bottom.

How Many People Will Be Invited to the Party?

It's very important to know the approximate number of people who will be invited, since this is the basis of the math you will do for everything related to the party. How else will you be able to calculate the amounts of food and drink, invitations, napkins, and glasses? This is especially important for a bar cart host because careful curation means you won't have a lot of backup spirits and mixers. Make a list, check it twice, and always invite the naughty and the nice for a memorable party.

These recipes cover seasons and holidays found in May, June, July, and August.

Blue Skyy Summer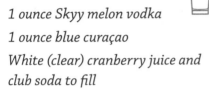

1 ounce Skyy melon vodka

1 ounce blue curaçao

White (clear) cranberry juice and club soda to fill

Pour the vodka and curaçao into a highball glass of ice. Fill with equal parts of white (clear) cranberry juice and club soda.

Born on the 4th of July Martini

1½ ounces cherry vodka or rum

3 ounces white (clear) cranberry juice

1 maraschino cherry

½ ounce blue curaçao

Combine the cherry vodka or rum and the white (clear) cranberry juice in a shaker with ice. Shake well. Strain into a cocktail glass. Drop the cherry in to sink to the bottom, then carefully float the blue curaçao on top by pouring it over the back of a spoon.

Canadian Crown (Canada Day)

2 ounces Crown Royal Canadian blended whisky

1 ounce lemon juice

½ ounce simple syrup

½ ounce grenadine

1 maraschino cherry

Combine the liquid ingredients in a shaker with ice. Shake well. Strain into a cocktail glass. Add the cherry.

Champagne Fountain

You can rent a champagne fountain at a local party store and pour in anything you want as long as it doesn't have pulp or seeds. Even though the fountain will have a chiller, it's best to pour in your chosen mixture when cold.

Cinco de Mayo Martini

1 ounce aged tequila

1 ounce coconut-flavored tequila

½ ounce agave liqueur

2 ounces lime juice

1 ounce simple syrup

Combine the ingredients in a shaker with ice. Shake well. Strain into a cocktail glass.

Horse's Neck (Kentucky Derby)

1 lemon rind spiral (historic bar garnish)
2 ounces Kentucky whiskey
Dash Angostura bitters
Ginger ale to fill

To make the horse's neck, simply slice into the top of a whole lemon and carefully peel the entire peel off in a spiral. Lower the spiral into a highball glass, then slowly add ice so that the horse's neck is spiraled all the way up the glass. Pour in the whiskey, dash of bitters, and fill with ginger ale.

Wedding Cake Martini

1 ounce vanilla vodka
½ ounce amaretto
½ ounce white chocolate liqueur
1 ounce cream

Combine the ingredients in a shaker with ice. Shake well. Strain into a cocktail glass.

Wedding Reception Bubbles

½ ounce strawberry vodka
1 ounce strawberry liqueur
Dry champagne to fill
1 strawberry, for garnish

Pour the strawberry vodka and the strawberry liqueur into a champagne flute and fill with champagne. Garnish the rim with a strawberry.

These recipes cover seasons and holidays found in September, October, November, and December.

Devil's Blood (Halloween)

¾ glass cranberry juice

2 ounces Blavod black vodka

Pack a highball glass with ice, then pour the cranberry juice three-quarters to the top. Slowly pour the black vodka on top.

Bloody Punch Bowl Hand

Make a bloody hand to float around in a Halloween punch from cranberry juice and a latex glove. Fill the glove with the juice, tie, freeze, then rip the glove off. Some gloves have talcum powder inside—make sure you rinse it out first.

The Grinch's Sour Caramel Apple Pie

Raw sugar and crushed graham crackers, for rimming

1 ounce cream

1 ounce green apple vodka or rum

1 ounce sour apple schnapps

1 ounce butterscotch schnapps

Cinnamon, for sprinkling

In a saucer, mix raw sugar and graham crackers; wet the rim of a cocktail glass with cream and dip it into the sugared crumbs. Shake the remaining liquid ingredients, including the remaining cream, with ice and strain into the cocktail glass. Sprinkle with cinnamon.

Holly Berry

1½ ounces raspberry vodka

½ ounce triple sec

¼ ounce Rose's lime juice

3 ounces cranberry juice

Washed holly sprig without berries, or plastic replica (optional)

Combine the liquid ingredients in a shaker with ice. Shake well. Strain into a cocktail glass. Garnish with the washed holly sprig without the berries for a festive touch. (Don't eat the berries—they are toxic.)

Hot Gingerbread Toddy

½ cup water

1" knob ginger, thinly sliced

⅛ cup sugar

1 ounce light rum

1 cup hot apple cider

Combine the water and ginger in a saucepan and bring to a boil. Remove from heat. Cover and steep 30 minutes. Add the sugar and boil again, stirring until the sugar dissolves. Strain ¼ cup into an Irish coffee mug, then add the rum. Fill with hot apple cider.

Pumpkin Pie

Raw sugar and nutmeg, for rimming

1 ounce cream

2 ounces vanilla vodka

1 ounce pumpkin schnapps

In a saucer, mix a little raw sugar (the brown kind) and nutmeg; then wet the rim of a cocktail glass with cream and dip the glass into the sugar and spice. Shake the rest of the ingredients, including the remaining cream, with ice and strain into a cocktail glass.

Thanksgiving Turkey Cosmo

1½ ounces Wild Turkey bourbon

½ ounce triple sec

¼ ounce lime juice

2 ounces cranberry juice

Combine the ingredients in a shaker with ice. Shake well. Strain into a cocktail glass.

15. Mocktails (Nonalcoholic Drinks)

*M*ocktails are exactly what they sound like—mock cocktails. They are also called nonalcoholic drinks, alcohol-free drinks, or virgin drinks. In their most basic form, simply omitting the alcohol from a cocktail will create a mocktail. However, you want to be a little more creative than just leaving the vodka out of a Screwdriver.

There are countless reasons to select a mocktail, including pregnancy, being the designated driver, taking certain medications, dislike of alcohol, being under drinking age, personal choice, or allergies. A good host always keeps a few mocktail recipes on hand so all guests can feel welcome and comfortable.

Mocktails can be frozen, juicy, creamy, sour, sweet, hot, fizzy, spicy, or any other category, just like regular cocktails. They can be made with veggies (such as cucumbers), herbs, nonalcoholic wine, rum extracts, flavored syrups, and just about anything else you can imagine.

The mixing of mocktails can easily be accomplished from your bar cart. Most of these drinks use mixers you will already have on hand, such as various kinds of fruit juices and sodas. Then, just pick a syrup with a flavor that can combine with many of those mixers (such as raspberry syrup) and you'll be serving delicious mocktails from your bar cart with ease.

Arnold Palmer

Equal parts of lemonade and unsweetened tea to fill

1 lemon wedge, for garnish

Fill a highball glass with ice, then fill with equal parts of lemonade and unsweetened tea. Garnish with lemon wedge.

The Most Famous Mocktail

The most famous mocktail is called a Shirley Temple (today, people also call it a Kiddie Cocktail or a Cherry Sprite). It was named after the famous child actress from the 1930s and is believed to be created by a Hollywood bartender from Chasen's restaurant. The Shirley Temple consists of ginger ale and grenadine garnished with a maraschino cherry.

Beach Blanket

4 ounces white grape juice

3 ounces cranberry juice

Club soda to fill

Slice of lemon, slice of lime, and a cherry, for garnish (optional)

Pour the juices into a highball glass over ice. Add the club soda to fill. Stir gently. Garnish with lemon, lime, and cherry, if desired.

California Lite

3 ounces limeade

3 ounces lemonade

Club soda to fill

Orange slice, lemon slice, and cherry for garnish

Pour the limeade and lemonade into a highball glass over ice. Stir. Add the club soda to fill. Garnish with an orange slice, a lemon slice, and a cherry, if desired.

Canadian Cherry

2 ounces cherry soda

1 ounce orange juice

1 teaspoon lemon juice

Cherry, for garnish (optional)

Pour the liquid ingredients into an old-fashioned glass over ice. Stir well. Garnish with cherry if desired.

The Runner-Up Mocktail

The Roy Rogers is probably the second most popular mocktail. It came out in the 1950s and consists of cola and grenadine (Cherry Coke) garnished with a maraschino cherry. Its namesake was a clean-cut, strait-laced singing cowboy with his own TV show in the 1950s.

Caped Cod

Equal parts of cranberry juice and limeade to fill

Fill a highball glass with ice, then fill with equal parts of cranberry juice and limeade.

Cherry Bubbles

½ ounce grenadine

5 ounces sparkling cider

1 cherry, for garnish (optional)

Pour the liquid ingredients into a champagne flute. Garnish with the cherry if desired.

Chocolate-Dipped Strawberry

1 tablespoon chocolate or white chocolate syrup

1 ounce light cream

Strawberry soda to fill

Pour the chocolate and cream into a highball glass. Stir. Fill the glass with ice and soda.

Cowboy Will's

1½ ounces orange juice

½ ounce tonic

1 teaspoon fine sugar

Combine the ingredients in a shaker nearly filled with ice. Shake well. Strain into a cocktail glass.

Down the Rabbit Hole

3 ounces carrot juice

3 ounces pineapple juice

Sparkling cider to fill

Fill a highball glass with ice, then add the juices. Fill with sparkling cider.

Earth Angel Sangria

¾ glass grape juice or nonalcoholic red wine

Soda water to fill

Orange wheel, lime wheel, pineapple slice, and cherry, for garnish (optional)

Fill a highball glass three-quarters full with grape juice or nonalcoholic red wine. Fill with soda water. Garnish with orange wheel, lime wheel, pineapple slice, and cherry if desired.

Faux Kir Royale

1 ounce raspberry syrup

Chilled sparkling white grape juice to fill

1 lemon twist, for garnish

Pour the raspberry syrup into a champagne flute. Fill with the sparkling white grape juice. Garnish with lemon twist.

Syrups for Mocktails

Torani and Monin syrups are the most popular beverage syrups on the market. They are prevalent in coffee shops. There are about sixty flavors, ranging from blood orange to mojito mint, including sugar-free alternatives. You'll find that they add a ton of flavor without any alcohol.

Friendly Frog

1 ounce lemon juice

1 teaspoon granulated sugar

3 ounces cold water

2 ounces orange juice

1 lemon wedge, for garnish

Pour the liquid ingredients into a highball glass nearly filled with ice. Stir well. Garnish with a lemon wedge.

Gentle Wave

1½ ounces pineapple juice

1½ ounces cranberry juice

Splash orange juice

1 teaspoon grenadine

4 ounces tonic water

1 lemon, lime, or orange slice and a cherry, for garnish

Pour all ingredients except tonic water and fruit garnish in a highball glass over ice. Stir well. Add tonic. Stir again. Garnish with fruit garnish if desired.

Hawaiian Lemonade

4 ounces lemonade

3 ounces pineapple juice

Pineapple slice and cherry, for garnish (optional)

Pour the lemonade and pineapple juice in highball glass over ice. Garnish with fruit if desired.

Hot Clamato

6 ounces Clamato juice

1 ounce fresh lime juice

¼ teaspoon horseradish

Dash Tabasco sauce

Dash Worcestershire sauce

1 lemon wedge, for garnish

Pour the liquid ingredients into a highball glass over ice; stir. Garnish with lemon.

Tabasco Facts

Tabasco, the popular hot sauce, comes from Avery Island, 140 miles west of New Orleans. Tabasco has been produced since 1868. A 2-ounce bottle contains at least 720 drops.

Italian Cream Soda

1 ounce hazelnut syrup

Club soda to fill

Whipped cream, for garnish (optional)

Pour the hazelnut syrup into a highball glass of ice. Fill with club soda. Top with whipped cream if desired.

Juicy Julep

1 ounce lime juice

1 ounce pineapple juice

½ ounce raspberry syrup

2 sprigs of mint (reserve 1 for garnish)

Club soda to fill

Combine the first three ingredients and 1 mint sprig in a shaker half filled with ice. Shake well. Strain into a highball glass of ice. Add club soda and stir gently. Garnish with the remaining sprig of mint.

Lemony Apple

3 ounces apple juice

1 ounce lemon juice

8 ounces ginger ale

1 ounce grenadine

Pour the apple and lemon juices into a highball glass. Stir. Add the ginger ale. Drizzle in the grenadine.

Liberated Cuba Libre

Equal parts of cola and limeade to fill

1 lime wedge, for garnish

Fill a highball glass with ice, then fill with equal parts of cola and limeade. Garnish with lime wedge.

Mimi's Mimosa

2 ounces orange juice

Chilled sparkling white grape juice to fill

Pour the orange juice into a champagne flute. Fill with the sparkling white grape juice.

Mulled Cranberry Juice

6 ounces cranberry juice

Splash fresh lemon juice

1 teaspoon honey or more to taste

2 whole cloves

Dash nutmeg

Combine the ingredients in a saucepan and heat to simmer. Do not boil. Stir well. Pour into an Irish coffee mug.

Pineapple Sparkler

4 ounces pineapple juice

1 teaspoon fine sugar

Club soda or sparkling water

1 lemon or lime wedge, for garnish

Combine the juice and sugar in a shaker half filled with ice. Shake well. Strain into a white wine glass. Add soda to fill. Garnish with lemon or lime wedge.

Pink Pineapple

4 ounces pineapple juice

3 ounces cherry soda

1 tablespoon honey

1 ounce cream

Dash grenadine

Pour the ingredients into a highball glass of ice. Stir.

Planter's Punch (nonalcoholic)

2 ounces pineapple juice

3 ounces orange juice

1 ounce lemon juice

½ ounce grenadine

Fruit, for garnish

Combine the liquid ingredients in a shaker half filled with ice. Shake well. Strain into a highball glass of ice. Garnish with fruit. This is the nonalcoholic version of the rum-flavored punch of the same name.

15. MOCKTAILS (NONALCOHOLIC DRINKS)

Sweet Spice

1 ounce fresh lemon juice

3 ounces fresh orange juice

½ ounce grenadine

Ginger ale to fill

Cherries, for garnish (optional)

Fill a highball glass with ice and add the juices and grenadine. Fill with ginger ale. Garnish with cherries if desired.

Sweet Sunrise

Orange juice to fill

½ ounce grenadine

1 orange slice, for garnish

Fill a highball glass with ice, then fill with orange juice. Slowly pour the grenadine into the drink. It will sink to the bottom of the glass, making it look like a sunrise. Garnish with orange slice.

Virgin Island Seabreeze

1 part pink grapefruit juice

1 part cranberry juice

1 lime slice, for garnish

Fill a highball glass with ice. Pour in equal amounts of the pink grapefruit juice and cranberry juice. Garnish with slice of lime.

APPENDIX A.
Homemade Recipes

HOMEMADE BARREL-AGED SPIRITS AND COCKTAILS

HOMEMADE LIQUEURS

*M*aking your own syrups, mixes, infusions, and liqueurs is fun and can give a personal touch to your hosting. What matches the bar cart ethos better than to create your own individual mixers? It's all about selecting what is just right for you and your guests. Making your own mixers can let you create wonderful personalized gifts as well. Why not create a theme basket around your choice? This is truly a gift that can't be bought.

You'll discover that in order to make these homemade recipes you'll need a few things you don't normally have in the drawers and cabinets in your kitchen. The recipes included in this chapter may ask for filters. Sieves, mesh, cheesecloth, paper towels, and coffee filters will all work. You will also need wide-mouthed jars with tight, secure lids (such as canning jars), bottles (plain or decorative), gallon containers, saucepans, measuring spoons and cups, plastic bags, a funnel, and corks. Make sure everything is scrubbed, sanitized, and squeaky clean before starting—especially your hands!

HOMEMADE SYRUPS

When you mix a spoonful of sugar in iced tea, the sugar granules sink to the bottom of the glass. This is the reason why syrups mix better in cocktails. Fresh syrups are easy to make at home, so there is no need to buy bottles at the store that are filled with additives and preservatives. Once you learn how to make basic simple syrup from sugar, Splenda, honey, agave, or maple syrup, then you can let your imagination run wild with a variety of added flavors from fruits, vegetables, and herbs.

Making a Simple Syrup

A simple syrup is made with equal parts water and sugar. Bring the water to boil in a saucepan, then stir in the sugar until dissolved. Remove from heat and cool for 1 hour. Then strain into a sterilized container. For variations on this theme the recipe steps are the same, it is just the ingredients that differ. Try:

Agave syrup: equal parts water and agave

Honey syrup: equal parts water and Grade A honey

Maple syrup: equal parts water and Grade B maple syrup

Sugar-free syrup: equal parts water and Splenda

Flavored Syrups

To make flavored syrup, combine flavored water from fruit, vegetables, spices, and herbs with the sweetener of your choice.

Ginger Agave Syrup

½ cup sliced fresh ginger

1 cup water

1 cup agave

Bring the ginger and water to a boil, then strain. Pour the water back into the pot and stir in the agave until dissolved. Remove from heat and allow to cool for 1 hour. Strain into a sterilized container or bottle.

Ginger Maple Syrup

½ cup sliced fresh ginger

1 cup water

1 cup maple syrup

Bring the ginger and water to a boil, then strain. Pour the water back into the pot and stir in the maple syrup until dissolved. Remove from heat and allow to cool for 1 hour. Strain into a sterilized container or bottle.

Ginger Syrup

½ cup sliced fresh ginger

1 cup water

1 cup sugar

Bring the ginger and water to a boil, then strain. Pour the water back into the pot and stir in the sugar until dissolved. Remove from heat and allow to cool for 1 hour. Strain into a sterilized container or bottle.

Oxygen Deprivation

Oxygen might be crucial for you to live, but it will kill your creations. It's very important that all containers have tight, secure lids. Once your creations are made, continue to keep the air out by making sure you have a tight seal on your bottle. Lots of people like to use corks. You can buy them at hobby stores and sites online.

Ginger Syrup (sugar-free)

½ cup sliced fresh ginger

1 cup water

1 cup Splenda

Bring the ginger and water to a boil, then strain. Pour the water back into the pot and stir in the Splenda until dissolved. Remove from heat and allow to cool for 1 hour. Strain into a sterilized container or bottle.

Grenadine

1 cup pomegranate juice

1 cup sugar

Bring juice to a simmer and add the sugar. Stir until dissolved, then remove from heat and allow to cool. Pour into a sterilized bottle or container.

Sweet Potato Syrup

2 medium sweet potatoes

Few whole cloves (optional)

1 cinnamon stick (optional)

1 cup sugar (raw, brown, or white)

1. Juice the sweet potatoes in a centrifugal juicer and allow to stand for 1 hour so the starch settles to the bottom. Fine-strain the juice three times, and then measure out 1 cup and add to a medium pot and heat over medium heat.

2. Add a few whole cloves and a cinnamon stick if desired. Stir in the sugar until dissolved.

3. Remove from heat, fine-strain, and allow to cool for an hour. Strain into a sterilized container or bottle.

Tea Syrup

1 bag of tea (flavor of your choice)

1 cup water

1 cup sugar

Bring the tea bag and water to a boil in a medium pot, and then remove the tea bag. Stir in the sugar until dissolved. Remove from heat and allow to cool for an hour. Strain into a sterilized container or bottle.

The Law

In case you were wondering, you are not allowed to distill your own alcohol without a license. However, you are allowed to make as much homemade wine, liqueur, or beer as you wish. You just cannot sell it. But you can share it, so go ahead and get started!

Herb Syrups

Use the basics of making fresh mint syrup to substitute a fresh herb of your choice. Try basil, thyme, jasmine, lemongrass, lavender, parsley, cilantro, rosemary, sage, etc.

Mint Agave Syrup

½ cup fresh mint leaves

1 cup water

1 cup agave

Bring the mint and water to a boil, then strain. Pour the water back into the pot and stir in the agave until dissolved. Remove from heat and allow to cool for 1 hour. Strain into a sterilized container or bottle.

Mint Honey Syrup

½ cup fresh mint leaves

1 cup water

1 cup Grade A honey

Bring the mint and water to a boil, then strain. Pour the water back into the pot and stir in the honey until dissolved. Remove from heat and allow to cool for 1 hour. Strain into a sterilized container or bottle.

Mint Maple Syrup

½ cup fresh mint leaves

1 cup water

1 cup Grade B maple syrup

Bring the mint and water to a boil, then strain. Pour the water back into the pot and stir in the maple syrup until dissolved. Remove from heat and allow to cool for 1 hour. Strain into a sterilized container or bottle.

Mint Syrup

½ cup fresh mint leaves

1 cup water

1 cup sugar (raw, brown, or white)

Bring the mint and water to a boil, then strain. Pour the water back into the pot and stir in the sugar until dissolved. Remove from heat and allow to cool for 1 hour. Strain into a sterilized container or bottle.

Mint Syrup (sugar-free)

½ cup fresh mint leaves

1 cup water

1 cup Splenda

Bring the mint and water to a boil, then strain. Pour the water back into the pot and stir in the Splenda until dissolved. Remove from heat and allow to cool for 1 hour. Strain into a sterilized container or bottle.

Fruit Syrups

Use the basics of making raspberry syrup to make other fruit syrups. Simply substitute a berry of your choice. Try blueberries, blackberries, huckleberries, or strawberries.

Raspberry Agave Syrup

1 pound fresh raspberries

2 cups water

1 cup agave

1. Bring the raspberries and water to a boil in a medium pot. Cook over medium heat for 20 minutes. Strain with a cheesecloth into another pot by squeezing out as much juice as you can, then discard the cheesecloth and raspberry pulp.

2. Bring your strained juice to a boil, add agave, and stir until dissolved. Simmer for 5 minutes; remove from heat and allow to cool for 1 hour. Strain into a sterilized container or bottle.

Raspberry Honey Syrup

1 pound fresh raspberries

2 cups water

1 cup Grade A honey

1. Bring the raspberries and water to a boil in a medium pot. Cook over medium heat for 20 minutes. Strain with a cheesecloth into another pot by squeezing out as much juice as you can, then discard the cheesecloth and raspberry pulp.

2. Bring your strained juice to a boil, add honey, and stir until dissolved. Simmer for 5 minutes; remove from heat and allow to cool for 1 hour. Strain into a sterilized container or bottle.

Raspberry Maple Syrup

1 pound fresh raspberries

2 cups water

1 cup maple syrup

1. Bring the raspberries and water to a boil in a medium pot. Cook over medium heat for 20 minutes. Strain with a cheesecloth into another pot by squeezing out as much juice as you can, then discard the cheesecloth and raspberry pulp.

2. Bring your strained juice to a boil, add maple syrup, and stir until dissolved. Simmer for 5 minutes; remove from heat and allow to cool for 1 hour. Strain into a sterilized container or bottle.

Raspberry Syrup

1 pound fresh raspberries

2 cups water

1 cup sugar

1. Bring the raspberries and water to a boil in a medium pot. Cook over medium heat for 20 minutes. Strain with a cheesecloth into another pot by squeezing out as much juice as you can, then discard the cheesecloth and raspberry pulp.

2. Bring your strained juice to a boil, add sugar, and stir until dissolved. Simmer for 5 minutes; remove from heat and allow to cool for 1 hour. Strain into a sterilized container or bottle.

Raspberry Syrup (sugar-free)

1 pound fresh raspberries

2 cups water

1 cup Splenda

1. Bring the raspberries and water to a boil in a medium pot. Cook over medium heat for 20 minutes. Strain with a cheesecloth into another pot by squeezing out as much juice as you can, then discard the cheesecloth and raspberry pulp.

2. Bring your strained juice to a boil, add Splenda, and stir until dissolved. Simmer for 5 minutes; remove from heat and allow to cool for 1 hour. Strain into a sterilized container or bottle.

Ancient Sherbet

The Chinese taught Arab traders how to combine syrups and snow to make sherbet. Arab traders showed the Venetians, and the Venetians showed the Romans.

Combination Syrups

Use the basics of making strawberry-mint syrup to make other combination syrups. Simply substitute a fruit-spice combination of your choice. Try peach-ginger, raspberry-vanilla, strawberry-peppercorn, apple-cinnamon, and more.

Strawberry-Mint Agave Syrup

1 pound fresh strawberries

1 cup mint leaves

3 cups water

1 cup agave

1. Bring the strawberries, mint, and water to a boil in a medium pot. Cook over medium heat for 20 minutes. Strain with a cheesecloth into another pot by squeezing out as much juice as you can, then discard the cheesecloth, strawberry pulp, and mint.

2. Bring your strained juice to a boil, add agave, and stir until dissolved. Simmer for 5 minutes; remove from heat and allow to cool for 1 hour. Strain into a sterilized container or bottle.

Strawberry-Mint Honey Syrup

1 pound fresh strawberries

1 cup mint leaves

3 cups water

1 cup Grade A honey

1. Bring the strawberries, mint, and water to a boil in a medium pot. Cook over medium heat for 20 minutes. Strain with a cheesecloth into another pot by squeezing out as much juice as you can, then discard the cheesecloth, strawberry pulp, and mint.

2. Bring your strained juice to a boil, add honey, and stir until dissolved. Simmer for 5 minutes; remove from heat and allow to cool for an hour. Strain into a sterilized container or bottle.

Strawberry-Mint Maple Syrup

1 pound fresh strawberries

1 cup mint leaves

3 cups water

1 cup maple syrup

1. Bring the strawberries, mint, and water to a boil in a medium pot. Cook over medium heat for 20 minutes. Strain with a cheesecloth into another pot by squeezing out as much juice as you can, then discard the cheesecloth, strawberry pulp, and mint.

2. Bring your strained juice to a boil, add maple syrup, and stir until dissolved. Simmer for 5 minutes; remove from heat and allow to cool for an hour. Strain into a sterilized container or bottle.

Strawberry-Mint Syrup

1 pound fresh strawberries

1 cup mint leaves

3 cups water

1 cup sugar

1. Bring the strawberries, mint, and water to a boil in a medium pot. Cook over medium heat for 20 minutes. Strain with a cheesecloth into another pot by squeezing out as much juice as you can, then discard the cheesecloth, strawberry pulp, and mint.

2. Bring your strained juice to a boil, add sugar, and stir until dissolved. Simmer for 5 minutes; remove from heat and allow to cool for 1 hour. Strain into a sterilized container or bottle.

Strawberry-Mint Syrup (sugar-free)

1 pound fresh strawberries

1 cup mint leaves

3 cups water

1 cup Splenda

1. Bring the strawberries, mint, and water to a boil in a medium pot. Cook over medium heat for 20 minutes. Strain with a cheesecloth into another pot by squeezing out as much juice as you can, then discard the cheesecloth, strawberry pulp, and mint.

2. Bring your strained juice to a boil, add Splenda, and stir until dissolved. Strain into a sterilized container or bottle.

Medicinal Mint

Mint has long been used as a medicinal herb, and it's still considered useful today for soothing upset stomachs.

Spice Syrups

Use the basics of making vanilla syrup to create spice syrups of your choice. Try anise, cinnamon sticks, fresh grated nutmeg, whole cloves, peppercorns, chilies, etc.

Vanilla Agave Syrup

3 vanilla beans, diced

1 cup water

1 cup agave

Bring the vanilla beans and water to a boil in a medium pot, then strain. Pour the water back into the pot and stir in the agave until dissolved. Remove from heat and allow to cool for an hour. Strain into a sterilized container or bottle.

Vanilla Honey Syrup

3 vanilla beans, diced

1 cup water

1 cup Grade A honey

Bring the vanilla beans and water to a boil in a medium pot, then strain. Pour the water back into the pot and stir in the honey until dissolved. Remove from heat and allow to cool for an hour. Strain into a sterilized container or bottle.

Vanilla Maple Syrup

3 vanilla beans, diced

1 cup water

1 cup Grade B maple syrup

Bring the vanilla beans and water to a boil in a medium pot, then strain. Pour the water back into the pot and stir in the maple syrup until dissolved. Remove from heat and allow to cool for an hour. Strain into a sterilized container or bottle.

Vanilla Syrup

3 vanilla beans, diced

1 cup water

1 cup sugar (raw, brown, or white)

Bring the vanilla beans and water to a boil in a medium pot, and then strain. Pour the water back into the pot and stir in the sugar until dissolved. Remove from heat and allow to cool for an hour. Strain into a sterilized container or bottle.

Vanilla Syrup (sugar-free)

3 vanilla beans, diced

1 cup water

1 cup Splenda

Bring the vanilla beans and water to a boil in a medium pot, and then strain. Pour the water back into the pot and stir in the Splenda until dissolved. Remove from heat and allow to cool for an hour. Strain into a sterilized container or bottle.

Fresh is always best. Once you taste a fresh cocktail made with fresh mix, you will never want to make another cocktail with artificial flavors and preservatives again. Sadly, generations born after 1960 have grown accustomed to inferior mixes that sit on store shelves. It's time to get back to freshness the way our great-grandmothers made everything decades ago.

Basic Bar Punch

Makes 1 gallon

3 cups fresh-squeezed orange juice

1 cup homemade grenadine

3 cups sweet-and-sour mix

3 cups pineapple juice

Water to fill

Pour all ingredients except the water into a gallon container. Fill the rest of the way with water, leaving enough room at the top for agitation. Mix.

Bloody Mary Mix

Makes 1 gallon

4 ounces lemon juice

8 ounces Worcestershire sauce

8 ounces A.1. sauce

4 ounces raw horseradish (optional)

1 heaping tablespoon celery seed

1 heaping tablespoon black peppercorns

2 (46-ounce) cans whole plum tomatoes

Water as needed

Tabasco sauce (optional)

1. Add the lemon juice, Worcestershire sauce, A.1. sauce, and horseradish, if using, into a large container.

2. Pour the celery seed and peppercorns in a blender and blend on high for 30 seconds, and then dump into the large container.

3. Fill the blender halfway with the whole plum tomatoes and then add water to fill. Blend on high for 10 seconds. Fine-strain into the container. Continue this step until all the tomatoes have been blended and strained.

4. Mix all ingredients, including Tabasco, if using, pour into sterilized jars or bottles, and refrigerate. You can add many types of ingredients to a basic Bloody Mary mix as you desire: beef bouillon cube, wasabi, garlic, avocado, chili powder, or bitters.

Cran-Apple Juice

Makes 1 (750-milliliter) bottle (about 25 ounces)

4 cups fresh cranberries

1 cup apple juice

Water to taste

Process the cranberries in a juicer. Mix together the cranberry juice and apple juice. Add water, little by little, and taste-test along the way until it reaches the desired tart-and-sweet balance. Refrigerate.

Cranberry Juice

Makes 1 (750-milliliter) bottle (about 25 ounces)

4 cups fresh cranberries

1 cup sugar

Water to taste

Process the cranberries in a juicer, and then pour into a widemouthed container with a lid. Add the sugar and shake until dissolved. Add water, little by little, and taste-test along the way until it reaches the desired tart-and-sweet balance. Refrigerate.

Cranberry Juice (sugar-free)

Makes 1 (750-milliliter) bottle (about 25 ounces)

4 cups fresh cranberries or frozen cranberries, thawed

1 cup Splenda

Water to taste

Process the cranberries in a juicer, and then pour into a widemouthed container with a lid. Add the Splenda and shake until dissolved. Add water, little by little, and taste-test along the way until it reaches the desired tart-and-sweet balance. Refrigerate.

The Cranberry

Cranberries are one of the three fruits that are native to North America. The other two are Concord grapes and blueberries.

APPENDIX A. HOMEMADE RECIPES

Ginger Beer

Makes 4 cups

1 large piece of ginger root, peeled

6 ounces simple syrup

4 ounces lemon juice, strained

20 ounces water

⅛ teaspoon yeast

Juice the ginger root until you get 2 ounces, and then add to a large bowl. Add the rest of the ingredients and stir. Funnel into a sterilized jar or bottle and allow to sit in the refrigerator for 2 days.

Margarita Mix

Makes 6 cups

2 cups fresh lime juice

2 cups simple syrup

2 cups water

Combine the ingredients in a large lidded container. Shake well. Adjust the amount of simple syrup and water according to your personal preference; refrigerate. Some people like this mix sweeter and others like it sourer. Keep taste-testing until you find your preference. This will only last 2 days.

Margarita Mix (sugar-free)

Makes 5 cups

2 cups fresh lime juice

2 cups sugar-free simple syrup

1 cup water

Combine the ingredients in a large lidded container. Shake well. Adjust the amount of simple syrup and water according to your personal preference; refrigerate. Some people like this mix sweeter and others like it sourer. Keep taste-testing until you find your preference. This will only last 2 days.

Piña Colada Mix

Makes 10 cups

1 (46-ounce) can pineapple juice (or homemade pineapple juice)

2 (15-ounce) cans Coco Lopez Cream of Coconut

6 drops vanilla extract

Blend the pineapple juice, coconut cream, and vanilla extract in a blender for 5 seconds, then refrigerate.

Pineapple Juice

Makes 10 ounces

1 ripe pineapple

2 tablespoons sugar

Dice the pineapple meat and place into a blender with the sugar. Blend for 10 seconds, and then fine-strain and refrigerate.

Strawberry Daiquiri Mix

Makes about 3 cups

2 cups unsweetened frozen strawberries, thawed

½ cup fresh lime juice

1 cup simple syrup

Blend the thawed strawberries, lime juice, and simple syrup in a blender. Adjust the amount of simple syrup and strawberries according to your personal preference. Refrigerate.

Strawberry Daiquiri Mix (sugar-free)

Makes about 3 cups

2 cups frozen strawberries, thawed

½ cup lime juice

1 cup sugar-free simple syrup

Blend the thawed strawberries, lime juice, and sugar-free simple syrup in a blender. Adjust the amount of simple syrup and strawberries according to your personal preference. Refrigerate.

Sweet-and-Sour Mix (often called Sour Mix)

Makes about 6 cups

2 cups lemon juice

½ cup lime juice

2 cups simple syrup

4 organic egg whites or equivalent amount of pasteurized egg whites or egg white substitute

1 cup water

Combine the ingredients together in a large lidded container. Shake well. Adjust the amount of simple syrup according to your personal preference, then refrigerate (it will keep for less than a day). Some people like this mix sweeter and others sourer. Keep taste-testing until you find your preference.

Sweet-and-Sour Mix (sugar-free)

Makes about 6 cups

2 cups fresh lemon juice

½ cup fresh lime juice

2 cups sugar-free simple syrup

4 organic egg whites or equivalent amount of pasteurized egg whites or egg white substitute

1 cup water

Combine the ingredients together in a large lidded container. Shake well. Adjust the amount of simple syrup according to your personal preference, then refrigerate. Some people like this mix sweeter and others sourer. Keep taste-testing until you find your preference.

HOMEMADE INFUSIONS

Commercial infusions and flavored spirits can often have a sweet chemical taste and smell. Making your own infusions is easy, because alcohol does a great job of extracting flavors from fruit, vegetables, spices, herbs, and fats. Give it a try!

Basic Infusion Recipe

Washed fruit, vegetable, spice, or herb of your choice

Vodka, gin, rum, tequila, brandy, or whiskey

Place your chosen fruit, vegetable, spice, or herb in a sterilized container. Add the alcohol and close the lid tightly. Remove from direct sunlight and let sit from 1 day to 2 weeks. Shake once a day. Strain and bottle when finished.

Start with Small Batches

There's no need to use full bottles of alcohol for infusing. Simply invest in some small canning jars or recycle mayonnaise and other jars. Make small batches with a cup or half bottle of spirit before investing in a large batch.

Infusing Times

Fruits, vegetables, spices, and herbs each have different infusing times because each has a different density and intensity of flavor. Some take a day and others take weeks. Here is a good time guideline to follow:

1-3 DAYS: Whole herbs, cracked spices, split vanilla beans, chopped hot peppers, dried fruit, and cracked coffee beans; **3-6 DAYS:** Whole berries, sliced stone fruits, sliced melons, sliced sweet peppers, and citrus zest/peels; **5-7 DAYS:** Chopped apples, chopped pears, sliced cucumbers, chopped mango, and chopped vegetables; **7-14 DAYS:** Skinned and sliced pineapple, peeled and diced ginger, and whole peppers.

Matching Spirit and Infusion

Certain flavors infuse better with particular spirits than others, the same way certain food flavors mix together well. Here are some guidelines for matching your infusions with spirits.

VODKA: Since vodka is basically a neutral grain spirit, it infuses well with any fruit, vegetable, spice, or herb of your choice.

GIN: Cucumber, apple, pear, citrus, lavender, fennel, basil, tea, berries, rosemary, lemongrass, rhubarb, and star anise.

LIGHT RUM: Light rum adapts to infusions much like vodka, so many flavors can be infused with light rum. Try pineapple, mango, papaya, lychee, dried coconut, and dates.

DARK RUM: Vanilla bean, cinnamon sticks, citrus, prunes, coffee beans, and chili peppers.

TEQUILA: Ginger, pineapple, citrus, hot peppers, mango, pomegranate seeds, berries, dried coconut, watermelon, and mint.

WHISKEY: Apples, cherries, figs, walnuts, cinnamon sticks, peaches, plums, mint, vanilla bean, orange zest, and ginger.

Bitters has been used for medicinal purposes for centuries, such as to aid digestive health. Historical cocktail books show that bitters also served as an essential ingredient in cocktails. A couple of dashes of bitters in a cocktail adds a bright burst of complex flavor. Bitters is made with barks, roots, herbs, seeds, fruits, spices, and vegetables, and then preserved with high-proof alcohol. Be creative! Use anise, allspice, thistle blossoms, celery seed, wormwood, and any fruit or vegetable desired. The combinations are unlimited.

Basic Bitters
Makes 16 ounces

1 cup dried bitter orange peel

Pinch cardamom

Pinch caraway

Pinch coriander seeds

2 cups grain alcohol

Combine all the ingredients into a sterilized jar with a lid and allow to sit in a cool, dark place for 20 days, agitating it every day. Strain through a coffee filter into another jar, and then transfer to dropper bottles or bitters bottles.

Buying Herbs and Other Bitters Ingredients
Herbs and other ingredients required for bitters, such as cherry bark, can be purchased from herb shops and natural food stores as well as from sellers online.

Bourbon Bitters

Makes 16 ounces

¼ cup roasted pecans

¼ cup roasted walnuts

1 cinnamon stick

2 whole cloves

1 vanilla bean, split

1 tablespoon cinchona bark

1 tablespoon wild cherry bark

1 tablespoon gentian root

2 cups high-proof bourbon

2 tablespoons maple syrup

Combine all the ingredients, except maple syrup, into a sterilized jar with a lid and allow to sit in a cool, dark place for 20 days, agitating it every day. Strain through a coffee filter into another jar. Add the maple syrup, stir, and then transfer to dropper bottles or bitters bottles.

Cocoa Bitters

Makes 16 ounces

½ cup cracked cocoa nibs

¼ cup orange peels

1 tablespoon wild cherry bark

½ cinnamon stick

2 cups high-proof rum

Combine all the ingredients into a sterilized jar with a lid and allow to sit in a cool, dark place for 20 days, agitating it every day. Strain through a coffee filter into another jar, and then transfer to dropper bottles or bitters bottles.

Coffee Bitters

Makes 16 ounces

½ cup cracked coffee beans

¼ cup orange peels

¼ cup cracked cacao nibs

½ cinnamon stick

2 cups grain alcohol

Combine all the ingredients into a sterilized jar with a lid and allow to sit in a cool, dark place for 20 days, agitating it every day. Strain through a coffee filter into another jar, and then transfer to dropper bottles or bitters bottles.

Orange Bitters

Makes 16 ounces

1 cup orange peels

1 teaspoon fennel seed

2 cardamom pods

Pinch coriander seeds

10 drops gentian extract

2 cups grain alcohol

Combine all the ingredients into a sterilized jar with a lid and allow to sit in a cool, dark place for 20 days, agitating it every day. Strain through a coffee filter into another jar, and then transfer to dropper bottles or bitters bottles.

In the 1600s, barrels were used to store wine because it caused less breakage than storing it in clay or glass containers. It also made transportation of the wine easier. In the 1700s, the insides of barrels were torched to create a layer of charcoal, and were then used to age whiskey. In 2010, the first people to entertain the idea of aging cocktails in charred white oak barrels were Tony Conigliaro and Jeffrey Morgenthaler, mixologists from London and Portland, Oregon, respectively. Today, it's common for craft cocktail bars to have barrel-aged cocktails listed on their menus.

Recipe Yields in This Section

The following recipes are for filling a 1-liter barrel. You'll need to adjust ingredient amounts and do the math to fill larger barrels.

You can barrel-age your own spirits and cocktails by buying a barrel and experimenting in the comfort of your own home. Barrel aging adds a deeper and softer flavor to spirits and cocktails. Depending on the size of your barrel, the average aging time is 6 weeks, but you need to taste-test throughout the aging period to determine when you should empty the contents of the barrel into sterilized bottles. The goal is to avoid a woody cocktail taste.

The preparation steps before using your barrel are easy: Rinse out the barrel with water. Fill the barrel with water, soaking it long enough so that the wood swells. Be sure to check for any leaks. Pour out the water. Allow the barrel to dry. You are now ready to funnel in your chosen cocktail or spirit.

Barrel-Aged B and B

16 ounces brandy

16 ounces Bénédictine

Funnel the ingredients into the barrel for aging. Roll the barrel once a day. Bottle contents before your ingredients begin to taste woody.

Barrel-Aged Bijou

11 ounces gin

11 ounces green Chartreuse

11 ounces sweet vermouth

11 dashes orange bitters

Funnel the ingredients into the barrel for aging. Roll the barrel once a day. Bottle contents before your ingredients begin to taste woody.

Barrel-Aged Black Russian

21 ounces vodka

11 ounces coffee liqueur

Funnel the ingredients into the barrel for aging. Roll the barrel once a day. Bottle contents before your ingredients begin to taste woody.

Barrel-Aged Chrysanthemum

20 ounces dry vermouth

10 ounces Bénédictine

2 ounces absinthe

Funnel the ingredients into the barrel for aging. Roll the barrel once a day. Bottle contents before your ingredients begin to taste woody.

Barrel-Aged El Presidente

20 ounces rum

5 ounces orange curaçao

5 ounces dry vermouth

1 ounce grenadine

Funnel the ingredients into the barrel for aging. Roll the barrel once a day. Bottle contents before your ingredients begin to taste woody.

Barrel-Aged Godfather

16 ounces amaretto

16 ounces Scotch

Funnel the ingredients into the barrel for aging. Roll the barrel once a day. Bottle contents before your ingredients begin to taste woody.

Barrel-Aged Godmother

16 ounces amaretto

16 ounces vodka

Funnel the ingredients into the barrel for aging. Roll the barrel once a day. Bottle contents before your ingredients begin to taste woody.

Barrel-Aged Manhattan

21 ounces rye whiskey

11 ounces sweet vermouth

10 dashes Angostura or Abbott's bitters (or your own homemade bitters)

Funnel the ingredients into the barrel for aging. Roll the barrel once a day. Bottle contents before your ingredients begin to taste woody.

Barrel-Aged Last Word

11 ounces gin

11 ounces Luxardo maraschino liqueur

11 ounces green Chartreuse

Funnel the ingredients into the barrel for aging. Roll the barrel once a day. Bottle contents before your ingredients begin to taste woody. When making your cocktail, you will use 3 ounces of the Barrel-Aged Last Word and 1 ounce lime juice. Shake and strain into a chilled cocktail glass.

Previously Used Barrels

It is a common practice to age alcohol in previously used barrels. Some tequilas are aged in used Jack Daniel's barrels, some Scotches are aged in used sherry barrels, and some beers are aged in used wine barrels. While aging, some of the taste of what was aged before seeps into the new batch. So why not try aging your own con- coctions in a previously used barrel to gain similar results?

Barrel-Aged Martini

21 ounces gin

11 ounces dry vermouth

Funnel the ingredients into the barrel for aging. Roll the barrel once a day. Bottle contents before your ingredients begin to taste woody.

Barrel-Aged Rob Roy

21 ounces Scotch

11 ounces sweet vermouth

10 dashes Angostura bitters

Funnel the ingredients into the barrel for aging. Roll the barrel once a day. Bottle contents before your ingredients begin to taste woody.

Barrel-Aged Rusty Nail

21 ounces Scotch

11 ounces Drambuie

Funnel the ingredients into the barrel for aging. Roll the barrel once a day. Bottle contents before your ingredients begin to taste woody.

Barrel-Aged Stinger

21 ounces cognac

11 ounces white crème de menthe

Funnel the ingredients into the barrel for aging. Roll the barrel once a day. Bottle contents before your ingredients begin to taste woody.

If you are giving your loved ones homemade liqueurs as gifts, try to make them extra special by hunting for special bottles at local thrift stores, antique stores, or the Internet; attaching a cocktail recipe to the bottle; or making a basket filled with needed glassware.

Amaretto

Makes 1 (750-milliliter) bottle (about 25 ounces)

2 cups sugar

1 cup brown sugar

2 cups water

3 cups vodka

¼ cup almond extract

4 teaspoons vanilla extract

Heat sugars and water until boiling and sugars are dissolved. Remove from heat and allow to cool. Add vodka, almond extract, and vanilla extract. Pour into a bottle and seal.

Coffee Liqueur

Makes 1 (750-milliliter) bottle (about 25 ounces)

4 cups sugar

1 cup brown sugar

5 cups water

1 cup instant coffee granules

5 tablespoons vanilla extract

½ of a 750-milliliter bottle premium vodka

Heat the sugars and the water until mixture boils. Stir until all sugar is dissolved. Remove from heat. Let cool to room temperature. Mix the sugar water, instant coffee, vanilla extract, and vodka together. Bottle the mixture and let it sit undisturbed in a cool, dark place for at least 1 month.

Faux Aquavit

Makes 1 (750-milliliter) bottle
(about 25 ounces)

1 (750-milliliter) bottle potato vodka

2 teaspoons caraway seeds

2 teaspoons dill seeds

2 star anise

2 teaspoons cumin seeds

1 teaspoon fennel seeds

1 teaspoon coriander seeds

1 whole clove

1 cinnamon stick

Pour the vodka into a jar and add the rest of the ingredients. Seal tightly and shake. Store in a cool, dark place for 2 to 3 weeks, shaking every 3 or 4 days. Strain and bottle: it is ready to drink. Place in the freezer to keep fresh.

Faux Drambuie

Makes 1 (750-milliliter) bottle
(about 25 ounces)

⅔ of a 750-milliliter bottle premium blended Scotch whisky

1 teaspoon fresh chopped rosemary

1 cup honey

Pour the Scotch into a widemouth jar. Add the rosemary. Cover and let stand for 24 hours, then strain into another jar. Add honey and shake the mixture. Let age in a dark place for 2 to 3 weeks. Strain through a coffee filter and pour into a clean bottle.

Faux Galliano

Makes 1 (750-milliliter) bottle (about 25 ounces)

3 cups filtered water

2 cups sugar

1 cup white Karo corn syrup

1 (750-milliliter) bottle 100 proof premium vodka

6 drops anise extract

3 drops banana extract

1 split vanilla pod

2 or 3 drops yellow food coloring

Boil water and sugar for 5 minutes to make a simple syrup. Remove from heat and let cool. Add Karo syrup, vodka, anise extract, and banana extract. Stir thoroughly, then pour into a widemouthed container and drop in the split vanilla pod. Let sit for 24 hours in a dark place. Strain into a sterilized bottle and add food coloring.

Faux Pimm's No. 1

Makes 1 (750-milliliter) bottle (about 25 ounces)

14 ounces premium gin

1 ounce Cointreau

7 ounces sweet vermouth

3 ounces sweet sherry or ruby port

Pour all ingredients into a clean 750-milliliter bottle. Cap or cork. Turn over once or twice and it's ready to serve.

Faux Tia Maria

Makes 1 (750-milliliter) bottle
(about 25 ounces)

4 cups sugar

1 cup brown sugar

5 cups water

1 cup instant coffee granules

5 tablespoons vanilla extract

*½ of a 750-milliliter bottle of
premium rum*

Heat the sugars and the water in
a medium pot until mixture boils.
Stir until all sugar is dissolved.
Remove from heat and let cool
to room temperature. Mix the
sugar water, instant coffee,
vanilla extract, and rum together.
Bottle the mixture and let it sit
undisturbed in a cool, dark place
for at least 1 month.

Irish Cream

Makes 1 (750-milliliter) bottle
(about 25 ounces)

¾ cup Irish whiskey

*1 (14-ounce) can sweetened
condensed milk*

1 cup whipping cream

4 eggs

*2 tablespoons chocolate-flavored
syrup*

2 teaspoons instant coffee granules

1 teaspoon vanilla extract

Blend all ingredients until
smooth. Store in a tightly covered
container in the refrigerator. It
can be served within 24 hours
and will last for 1 month. Always
stir before serving.

Limoncello

Makes 1 (750-milliliter) bottle
(about 25 ounces)

Zest from 7 organic lemons

1 (750-milliliter) bottle vodka

1 cup simple syrup

Wash the lemons well, then zest. Pour half of the vodka in a gallon glass jar and add zest. Cover and let sit at room temperature for 20 days. Add the simple syrup and remaining vodka and let sit for another 20 days. Strain and bottle: it is now ready to drink. Place in the freezer to keep fresh.

Mead

Makes 4 (750-milliliter) bottles
(about 25 ounces each)

1 gallon water

2½ pounds honey

Juice from 1 lemon

½ tablespoon nutmeg

1 package ale or champagne yeast

Boil the water and honey. Add the lemon juice and nutmeg. Skim the foam that rises to the surface. Remove from heat and cool to room temperature. Add the yeast. Cover and let sit at room temperature for 15–17 days—any longer and the yeast will make the mixture explosive. Bottle in glass containers with tight lids or corks and age for 2 weeks. Refrigerate.

Orangecello

Makes 1 (750-milliliter) bottle
(about 25 ounces)

*Zest from 7 organic navel oranges
(thick skinned)*

1 (750-milliliter) bottle vodka

1 cup simple syrup

Wash the oranges well, then zest. Pour half of the vodka in a gallon glass jar and add the zest. Cover and let sit at room temperature for 20 days. Add the simple syrup and remaining vodka and let sit for another 20 days. Strain and bottle: it is now ready to drink. Place in the freezer to keep fresh.

Peppermint Schnapps

Makes 1 (750-milliliter) bottle
(about 25 ounces)

⅔ cup granulated sugar

4 cups corn syrup

4 cups vodka

1½ tablespoons peppermint extract

Combine the sugar and corn syrup in a saucepan over medium heat until sugar dissolves. Remove from heat. Allow mixture to cool. Add the vodka and peppermint extract. Pour in a bottle and seal. To make cinnamon, root beer, or any other flavored schnapps, simply use that flavored extract instead of the peppermint.

Raspberry Liqueur

Makes about 2½ cups

1 pint fresh raspberries

2½ cups vodka

1 vanilla bean

¼ teaspoon whole allspice

½ cup simple syrup

Wash berries and lightly crush to release flavor. Place berries in a large-mouthed bottle and add vodka, vanilla bean, and allspice. Stir and store in a bottle in a cool, dark place for 3 weeks. Strain mixture through a cheesecloth and squeeze as much juice as possible from the pulp. Pour back in bottle and add simple syrup to taste. Age another 3 to 5 weeks.

Presidential Raspberries

George Washington cultivated raspberries in his garden at Mount Vernon; they were mostly used in desserts.

APPENDIX B.

U.S./Metric Conversion Chart

U.S. Volume Measure	Metric Equivalent
⅛ teaspoon	0.5 milliliter
¼ teaspoon	1 milliliter
½ teaspoon	2 milliliters
1 teaspoon	5 milliliters
½ tablespoon	7 milliliters
1 tablespoon (3 teaspoons)	15 milliliters
2 tablespoons (1 fluid ounce)	30 milliliters
¼ cup (4 tablespoons)	60 milliliters
⅓ cup	90 milliliters
½ cup (4 fluid ounces)	125 milliliters
⅔ cup	160 milliliters
¾ cup (6 fluid ounces)	180 milliliters
1 cup (16 tablespoons)	250 milliliters
1 pint (2 cups)	500 milliliters
1 quart (4 cups)	1 liter (about)
U.S. Weight Measure	**Metric Equivalent**
½ ounce	15 grams
1 ounce	30 grams
2 ounces	60 grams
3 ounces	85 grams
¼ pound (4 ounces)	115 grams
½ pound (8 ounces)	225 grams
¾ pound (12 ounces)	340 grams
1 pound (16 ounces)	454 grams

VOLUME CONVERSIONS

WEIGHT CONVERSIONS

Degrees Fahrenheit	Degrees Celsius
200 degrees F	95 degrees C
250 degrees F	120 degrees C
275 degrees F	135 degrees C
300 degrees F	150 degrees C
325 degrees F	160 degrees C
350 degrees F	180 degrees C
375 degrees F	190 degrees C
400 degrees F	205 degrees C
425 degrees F	220 degrees C
450 degrees F	230 degrees C

OVEN TEMP CONVERSIONS

American	Metric
8 x 1½ inch round baking pan	20 x 4 cm cake tin
9 x 1½ inch round baking pan	23 x 3.5 cm cake tin
11 x 7 x 1½ inch baking pan	28 x 18 x 4 cm baking tin
13 x 9 x 2 inch baking pan	30 x 20 x 5 cm baking tin
2 quart rectangular baking dish	30 x 20 x 3 cm baking tin
15 x 10 x 2 inch baking pan	30 x 25 x 2 cm baking tin (Swiss roll tin)
9 inch pie plate	22 x 4 or 23 x 4 cm pie plate
7 or 8 inch springform pan	18 or 20 cm springform or loose bottom cake tin
9 x 5 x 3 inch loaf pan	23 x 13 x 7 cm or 2 lb narrow loaf or pate tin
1½ quart casserole	1.5 liter casserole
2 quart casserole	2 liter casserole

BAKING PAN SIZES

Index

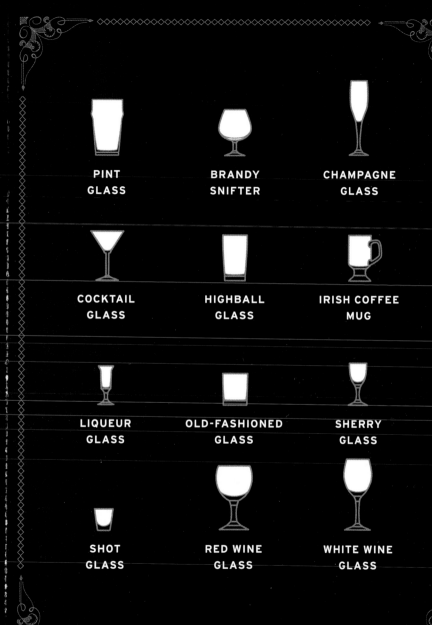

PINT
GLASS

BRANDY
SNIFTER

CHAMPAGNE
GLASS

COCKTAIL
GLASS

HIGHBALL
GLASS

IRISH COFFEE
MUG

LIQUEUR
GLASS

OLD-FASHIONED
GLASS

SHERRY
GLASS

SHOT
GLASS

RED WINE
GLASS

WHITE WINE
GLASS

•BARTENDER MEASURES•

MEASURE	STANDARD	METRIC
1 dash	0.03 ounce	0.9 milliliter
1 splash	0.25 ounce	7.5 milliliters
1 teaspoon	0.125 ounce	3.7 milliliters
1 tablespoon	0.375 ounce	11.1 milliliters
1 float	0.5 ounce	14.8 milliliters
1 pony	1 ounce	29.5 milliliters
1 jigger	1.5 ounces	44.5 milliliters
1 cup	8 ounces	237 milliliters
1 pint	16 ounces	472 milliliters
1 quart	32 ounces	946 milliliters
1 gallon	128 ounces	3.78 liters

POUR
ME
A
drink

here's to

alcohol

the rose colored

glasses of life

F. SCOTT FITZGERALD